ASLI ÇAVUŞOĞLU
The Place of Stone

Edited by Natalie Bell

NEW MUSEUM

Lead support provided by SAHA Association

Contents

ASLI ÇAVUŞOĞLU

Foreword

—

Lisa Phillips

In her research-driven practice, Aslı Çavuşoğlu takes up questions of history and belief by examining objects, images, and cultural symbols that have endured over time, or been fragmented or buried. National identity and the rhetoric used to construct political projects are concerns that recur throughout her works, resonating more deeply as nationalistic proclamations around the world take on an increasingly charged tenor. Many of Çavuşoğlu's works also address narratives of the past and suppositions of the present through oral histories, archives, artifacts, and raw materials, such as pigments derived from the natural world.

For her New Museum exhibition and residency, a partnership with the Istanbul-based SAHA Association, Çavuşoğlu has expanded her research into the histories of specific colors, exploring the origins and trade history of lapis lazuli, a blue stone that has been exported primarily from Afghan mines since the seventh century BC. The New Museum proudly debuted Çavuşoğlu's work in the United States in the 2015 New Museum Triennial: "Surround Audience," and we are now honored to host "The Place of Stone," her first solo museum exhibition in the US.

In her new body of work, Çavuşoğlu brings us to "the place of stone"—the translation of Sar-i Sang, the traditional name for the site of lapis mines in Afghanistan. She has created a beautiful wall of fresco panels, giving new life to the artistic form that has traditionally incorporated lapis pigment. As Çavuşoğlu's work reminds us, it is in frescoes that we find details of lapis lazuli's trade and distribution, as well as its cultural symbolism. In her installation in the New Museum's Lobby Gallery, the artist illustrates the remarkable history of blue across centuries and diverse geographies—from Central Asia to Africa to Europe—following its transitions and shifting associations, which span the sacred, the political, and the emotional.

This catalogue marks the most comprehensive monographic publication on Çavuşoğlu's work to date. Within these pages, independent curator and critic Amy Zion addresses the artist's approach to materials and histories at the fringes of knowledge; anthropologist and writer Michael Taussig muses on lapis lazuli and the relationships between color, language, and memory; artist Mariana Castillo Deball contributes a short story that serves as an allegory on the decay of objects and civilizations; and New Museum Associate Curator Natalie Bell speaks with Çavuşoğlu about what we find when we are seeking other things. We are grateful to the authors for their contributions, as well as to Dana Kopel, Senior Editor & Publications Coordinator at the New Museum, for carefully editing and overseeing the publication, and to Brendan Dugan and David Schoerner at An Art Service, for their design and care in ushering over a decade of the artist's work into this elegant publication.

At the New Museum, we wish to thank Natalie Bell for spearheading Çavuşoğlu's exhibition and catalogue, and bringing her work to our audiences. The exhibition is the result of the combined efforts of Ian Sullivan, Director of Exhibitions Management; Patrick Foran, Chief Preparator; Stephen Nunes, Production Preparator; and Abby Lepold, Registrar, who closely supported the exhibition's production and installation. We also wish to acknowledge the entire staff of the Museum and, in particular, Massimiliano Gioni, *Edlis Neeson Artistic Director*; Karen Wong, Deputy Director; and Diane Vivona, Acting Director of Development, along with their respective teams. Curatorial Assistant Francesca Altamura and curatorial intern Anna Hugo provided generous support throughout the preparation of the exhibition and publication.

Our deep gratitude extends first to SAHA Association for their lead support for Aslı Çavuşoğlu's residency and exhibition. Artist commissions at the New Museum are generously supported by the Neeson / Edlis Artist Commissions Fund, and the exhibition is also made possible with support provided by the Toby Devan Lewis Emerging Artists Exhibitions Fund. We are grateful to the Producers Council and the Artemis Council of the New Museum. Support for this publication has been provided by the J. McSweeney and G. Mills Publications Fund at the New Museum. We also extend special thanks to Naim and Özlem Gençoğlu for generously sponsoring the artist's studio space in Istanbul during a critical period of production, as well as to Füsun Eczacıbaşı and Merve Çağlar for their continued support of the artist's practice and this project in particular.

At the artist's studio, we are indebted to the assistance of Yavuz Parlar, who provided crucial support and project management. We are also grateful to Gülseren Dikillitaş, Şehrigül Erdek, Koray Erdek, İnci Eviner, Maya Kurdoğlu, Burak Ata, Sabo Akdağ, Cemil Aliyev, Taner Ceylan, Gürkan Çakır, Akif Kaynar, and Can Küçük for their skills and expertise in consulting on and supporting the realization and installation of the artist's fresco panels. Together with the artist, we wish to thank her parents, Meliha and Metin Çavuşoğlu, not merely for their encouragement, but for their practical hand in couriering kilos of pigment across borders and catering homemade lunches for the studio staff throughout the production of these works. It is impossible to imagine such an ambitious project without this dynamic and committed team.

Finally, we would like to extend our gratitude to Aslı Çavuşoğlu for bringing us this striking body of work and, with it, histories and colors that are equally rich and complex.

Lisa Phillips
Toby Devan Lewis Director, New Museum

Contrarian Blue: Aslı Çavuşoğlu at the New Museum

—

Amy Zion

Aslı Çavuşoğlu's exhibition "The Place of Stone" begins in a barren mountain range in what is today northern Afghanistan. There lies a deep, remote, and historic repository of lapis lazuli. The exhibition's title is a translation of Sar-e Sang, the historic name for this ancient mine, where a heavenly blue was forged beneath the earth through intense pressure and high temperature, swirling and binding lazurite to calcite and pyrite. This metamorphosis created a stone considered to be the first stable blue color discovered in nature. Its preciousness and beauty have never been undervalued: it has been traded throughout the world and is found throughout history, from the funerary mask of Tutankhamen to the walls of Giotto's frescoes in the Scrovegni Chapel in Padua to the exquisitely carved Buddhist hermit figures of the Qing Dynasty.

This raw material is the central motif of Çavuşoğlu's most recent research and body of work. Lapis, for the artist, runs like a tracer dye through histories and civilizations, connecting the artistic and religious traditions of disparate cultures and narrating histories of trade and conflict around the world. As a prized and sought-after stone once worth more by weight than gold, it is a material marker of the beloved, the divine, and the powerful: for millennia, lapis has been used to highlight subjects of importance or called upon in defense of the evil eye. And historically, the majority of lapis in the world today can be traced back to this one mine, Sar-e Sang.

For "The Place of Stone," Çavuşoğlu has designed a series of frescoes, working with fresco painters to execute them using traditional techniques and lapis pigment. The enormous, gridded wall painting she has produced illustrates the pigment's journey through time; its route from the depths of an ancient mine, along the great Khorasan Road, to the far reaches of the world; and its use in the material culture of countless civilizations from "before Christ" into the present. By tracing lapis's history through different epochs, craft traditions, and religious contexts, Çavuşoğlu not only sheds light on its past and its connections; she also gives form to what we do not perceive when we look at that shade of blue today.

In the West, blue became synonymous with religious piety during the cult of the Virgin as early as the fifth century, when the pigment was introduced to European painters, who used "Marian Blue" to color Mary's celestial, deep azure veil.[1] Today, blue marks the identity of the European Union, the United Nations, and NATO, as well as corporations like Facebook and Twitter—all entities that aim to convey a democratic ethos. Although more affordable synthetic pigments have largely supplanted the use of lapis in painting, the stone remains a coveted and valuable material. Sar-e Sang has been in full operation in spite of the region's conflicts; in fact, the mine figures into those conflicts, as profit from the sale of lapis funds arms dealing. Recent reports posit that since the US invasion in 2001, moreover, lapis has been looted from Sar-e Sang on an industrial scale, meaning that one of the country's most valuable exports produces little to no profit for the government and public interest.[2] Instead, reports have found that profits go directly to the Taliban, and may also be funding the Islamic State.[3] Çavuşoğlu locates her interest precisely in this evolution of use, status, and meaning— across time and space, and through culture and war, from sacred to commercial to "conflict mineral."

Çavuşoğlu has experience unraveling such vast and entangled narratives, and "The Place of Stone" extends her ongoing research on particular colors and their histories. In her work *Red / Red* (2015), the artist used the story of a significant pigment, Armenian red, produced from dried, ground Armenian cochineal insects, as a wedge to crack open a painful chapter of history that the Turkish government has preferred to keep shut. The insect is indigenous to the Ararat Plain, which spans parts of both Armenia and Turkey—a contentious border that is currently sealed as the two countries struggle to reconcile territorial disputes. Çavuşoğlu acquired twelve grams of the cochineal[4] and gave it to one of few people who knows how to extract the color from it,[5] then used the result to produce a series of drawings composed of only two pigments: the Armenian red from cochineal and Turkish red, derived from madder roots and later used (in a brighter, more industrial hue) for the Turkish flag.[6] Side by side, the bluer, paler Armenian red is dominated by the more saturated Turkish red, which pops out toward the viewer as the Armenian red recedes. These two reds, illustrating cultural symbols and patterns, act as proxy maps or abstract coda that stand in for the political turmoil between the two cultures, particularly since knowledge of the production of Armenian red abruptly cuts off after 1915.[7] Where language is not permitted and fails to heal historical wounds, Çavuşoğlu's project serves as another form of diplomatic relations—a diplomatic aesthetics, rather, which gives form to that which is perceptible through feeling and visual representation. Her work asserts that the two cultures have been forged side by side, in contact with each other, for centuries, regardless of present attitudes and circumstances.

Çavuşoğlu was born in 1982 in Istanbul, where she currently lives and works. Turkey's present political (sur)reality, as well as its modern history, is a consistent subject throughout her roughly fifteen years of artistic output, alongside a more general interest in unearthing the apocryphal chapters of world history. In 2011, she made her first budgeted film, *In Diverse Estimations Little Moscow*, following her graduation from the film academy at Marmara University; it centers on a repressed chapter of history that unfolded just prior to her birth. Until 2000 in Turkey, it was illegal to write about Point Operation, the military repression of a municipal direct democracy project that had begun in the left-leaning town of Fatsa in October 1979. On July 11, 1980, General Kenan Erven's military stormed the town, arresting, torturing, and persecuting thousands who were suspected of participating in this popular democratic movement. Çavuşoğlu learned of the events from her father, who grew up there; she spoke to local residents, gathering accounts of the violent events in which the military overthrew the town's mayor, quashed his attempts at fostering civic participation and self-governance, and killed at least fifty young revolutionaries in the mountains.[8] The suppression of open discussion of these events created fragmented testimonies, which Çavuşoğlu used to structure the film, shooting it on site with local people.

The film strings together a series of vignettes, reenacting stories, scenes, songs, and passages from banned literature related to the

coup. A man enters a wooded landscape and disappears into a
hole in the forest floor; an interior shot, lit by flame, reveals it to be
a hideout where fugitives hid for up to seven years. Another young
man runs across a mountainside and conceals himself inside a hol-
low tree, catching his breath. Inside a dance hall, a group of young
men introduces a kind of violent recital of a combat scene inside a
performance of traditional *dabke*, an Arab folk dance. These scenes
illustrate how an individual's memories, disconnected from a collective narrative (one which, in this case, would have been publicly
banned), grow in strange formations and become pocked within
repressive social and political climates. Speaking to residents of her
father's generation or older—who witnessed the events firsthand—
and connecting their accounts through theatrical interpretation
allows her to convey the ideological underpinnings of the clash as
well as the fears, excitement, and spirit of resistance that has been
excised from contemporary history lessons.

In a subsequent project titled *The Stones Talk* (2013), Çavuşoğlu
again took up apocryphal passages of history, but focused more
broadly on how certain narratives are privileged over others by
producing a kind of archaeological salon des refusés. She created
representations of seventy-one excavated objects that the Turkish
government deemed unfit for public display[9]: she selected a group
of these "B-list" objects, copying them first in their original materials
(such as bronze, ceramic, or glass) and then in a range of strikingly
contemporary materials like rubber, plastic, and foam. Çavuşoğlu
presented the new objects atop clusters of interconnected black
plinths, forming an experimental theater of things. This cast and
their arrangement, numbered from one to seventy-one without any
discernible logic, were relieved from the pressure to perform a specific script (there were no labels or descriptions). The objects were
subject only to the imaginations of those who encountered them,
who could conjure myriad tales about the people who might have
made these objects and the places in which they were found. In
The Stones Talk, the works on display are but a hint at the potential
stories one could weave from the countless objects in storage boxes
lining the walls of government institutions, never shown to the public.

The Stones Talk, like the other projects discussed here, is a
stand-in for something larger that cannot be perceived in full.
Midway through *In Diverse Estimations, Little Moscow*, the camera
pans across the torso and shoulders of a young woman with bright
blue nails, who holds a book covered with newspaper to conceal
its contents and reads (in part) a quotation that sounds like the
artist's own modus operandi:

> Bourgeois thinker Camus considers the universe to be
> absurd, inharmonious, irrational, and unknowable. In
> order to see this absurdity, the only thing you have to do is
> open your eyes and exert your reason. You can perceive
> facts with the help of science but you cannot perceive the
> universe. You can feel the tree, taste the water, and feel
> the wind; this is all you can have. Science will mention
> invisible galaxies formed by electrons gathered around
> a nucleus. This is only a hypothesis…

Çavuşoğlu's works address the mechanisms that structure
knowledge, but more so, they investigate the mechanisms and
circumstances that suppress it. Her project is to reveal that which
is hidden as much as it is about exploring the ways in which ideas,
events, people, and materials move on and off our radar, across time
and distance. She provides a glimpse of all that falls just outside
our comprehension by pinpointing small entry points, challenging
accepted histories, recuperating lost knowledge, and recovering
trade secrets. Çavuşoğlu's latest work, her frescos in "The Place of
Stone," is not meant to elucidate the entire history and present of
an ancient stone, with all the connections between world cultures,
religions, and economies that it encompasses. Instead, the frescoes
map lapis lazuli's unstable meanings throughout history, up to its
present, seemingly paradoxical associations with both democracy-
the-brand and international turmoil—but this is only a hypothesis…

1. Although scholars such as Michel Pastoureau contend that artists began to depict the Virgin Mary in blue after the twelfth century, the Virgin's association with the color blue, and specifically a shade known as "Marian Blue," is rooted in earlier Byzantine traditions. See Katy Kelleher, "Marian Blue, the Color of Angels, Virgins, and Other Untouchable Things," *The Paris Review*, March 6, 2018; and Pastoureau, *Blue: The History of a Color* (Princeton, NJ: Princeton University Press, 2018), 50.

2. See William A. Byrd and Javed Noorani, *Industrial-scale Looting of Afghanistan's Mineral Resources* (Washington, DC: United States Institute of Peace, 2017).

3. "The burgeoning phenomenon of industrial-scale looting of many Afghan mineral resources is extremely harmful to the country—strengthening and further entrenching power holders, corrupting the government and undermining governance, providing some funds to the Taliban and reportedly ISIS, and fueling both local conflicts and the wider insurgency. This dire situation calls for a multipronged and effective response." Ibid., 15.

4. The scientific name for these insects is *Porphyrophora hamelii*.

5. Armen Sahakyan, a phytotherapist, extracted the color using the traditional method, which dates back to the seventh century and is detailed in manuscripts from the fourteenth century.

6. The Ottomans used red flags for centuries, but the red flag of Turkey was adopted in 1844 and updated to its current version in 1936.

7. In 1915, the Ottomans killed roughly 1.5 million Armenians—the first modern genocide, which is still not recognized as such by Turkey. See *Encyclopedia Britannica Online*, s.v. "Armenian Genocide: Turkish-Armenian History," by Ronald Grigor Suny, accessed June 12, 2018, https://www.britannica.com/event/Armenian-Genocide.

8. Süreyyya Evren, "Direct Democracy in Fatsa," *Süreyyya Evren Yazılar* (blog), October 1, 2008, http://surmetinler.blogspot.com/2008/10/direct-democracy-in-fatsa.html.

9. Çavuşoğlu accessed these items through a friend working on a dig near the Greek border. She visited the site and photographed the process, observing the archaeologists' mode of classification before discovering that only about ten percent of what was found was determined to be useful; the rest was considered scraps. This process evidences the highly political aspect of archaeology—that there is a goal, a story to tell, which needs a specific cast to narrate it.

In the Time of Lapis Lazuli

—

Michael Taussig

Some quite other medium, you now want to say, when all along you had thought it was color, just color, good old color, useful for wrapping up reality as a gift. *Some quite other medium?* But what could it be, this curious light lightness that floats, that passes, that radiates across the valley like the breath of dying sun? What could it be? I choose to call it *polymorphous magical substance*. It affects all the senses, not just sight. It moves. It has depth and motion just as a stream has depth and motion, and it connects such that it changes whatever it comes into contact with. Or is it the other way around? That in changing, it connects? My immediate point of reference here, my strong image, is with something that leapt into my imagination several years ago, that inchoate light lightness likened to the feathers of newborn birds said to fill the bodies of Selk'nam Indian shamans on Isla Grande in the Beagle Channel of Tierra del Fuego at the tip of South America.[1]

Hard to imagine, this human body composed of feathers of newborn birds. Even harder to imagine is that this same stuff is profoundly implicated in the act of vision of the shamans and that such vision can cure as well as kill and is linked to communication with spirits active in dreams and song. We find this ethereal substance or something like it in many Indian societies in lowland South America and it has been likened by Claude Lévi-Strauss to *mana*, an auratic, sacred power emanating from persons and things and thought by the famous anthropologist Marcel Mauss to be the basis of all magic. One way of understanding this light lightness would be to liken it to human stem cells, with their potential to become any one of the highly specialized cells of the body—heart, brain, spine, liver, kidney, etc.—only here it is not the human body, but the body of the world.

Drawn from the mouth, this white, feathery substance lends itself to all manner of conjuring. It may condense into a small, spinning disc revolving at great speed as if alive in the palm of the hand, then be stretched to arm's length to be abruptly swallowed, despite its immense size.[2] It is like no substance we have ever seen or can imagine, more like a substance which is no substance, suspending laws of time and space where substance gives way to movement, manifesting itself in a myriad of changing forms. This, then, is what I call polymorphous magical substance, and it is how I prefer to think of color, something more than a spot of red or blue on a page.

Perhaps the story of ultramarine is helpful here. Before it was produced in factories in 1830, ultramarine was gotten from the semiprecious stone lapis lazuli in Afghanistan. Under the microscope, you can see why the natural and the synthetic varieties of ultramarine look different to the naked eye. While the synthetic pigment has homogeneous, round crystals that produce a consistent, all-the-same blue surface, the ultramarine derived from lapis lazuli has large, irregular crystals of varying transparency and, what is more, these crystals are clustered together with particles of mica, quartz, calcite, and pyrite, yielding what Anita Albus calls a color like the glittering firmament. The calcite crystals, she says, "sparkle like stars within the deep blue."[3]

Like fast food's effect on food, nineteenth-century color technology killed off the body of color and, as regards the fine arts as practiced by the likes of Jan van Eyck and Vermeer, choked off centuries of craft, notably the tremendous work of preparing pigments, fresh, each day; the underpainting or foundation of the painting; and, following that, the application of alternate layers of opaque colors and transparent varnishes, what Cézanne called the "secret soul of grounds" and others call "glazing." In enlargements of cross sections of paint samples from paintings made this way, what we see, says Albus, "would look like a landscape of geological layers of different shapes and colors."[4] Multilayering was the key and a crystalline, transparent density the result. You not only see it in Vermeer but also in the iridescent cloth woven by the Flemish and the Italians in the fifteenth century, no less than in the iridescence of a butterfly's wing. As Albus puts it, color is the *interplay* between *body* and *tone* (meaning hue). Each pigment a painter used had a different body, she writes, "which refracts, reflects, and absorbs light in a different way."[5]

But is not Anita Albus a shade too conservative with her language of the glittering firmament versus the all-the same-sameness of

synthetic paint? Is there not value in flat sameness, only we don't
see it as romance so much as the heroic mysteries of the void?
Take Yves Klein's *artificial* ultramarine, IKB, aka "International Klein
Blue," the resort to acronym telling you just how daringly industrial,
how daringly camp and modern this color is going to be, allowing
its progenitor to shock the 1950s art world with his ultramarine that
"literally takes on a life of its own," such that color "would become
the springboard for the space without limit."[6] If Albus's *natural* ultramarine plays with space like the flitting wings of the butterfly, the
spatial play of IKB is "vaporous, floating, timeless." But at the end of
the day, the butterfly seems a lot more fun, I would say. After all, IKB
is romantic too, for nothing is as romantic as being anti-romantic.

When we see a color, we are actually seeing a play with light in,
through, and on a body, the body of color itself. Being a matter
of texture, it is no wonder that color can seem to be what I call a
polymorphous magical substance, twisting itself as if alive through
the branches along with the dying sun. At least it would be of no
wonder were it not for changes in the production of paints since
the nineteenth century. "The very abundance of colors in the modern world," write François Delamare and Bernard Guineau quite
recently, "seems to dilute our relationship with them. We are losing
our intimate connection with the materiality of color, the attributes
of color that excite all the senses, not just sight."[7]

It is not by chance, Anita Albus says, that now "the language of
color nuances is always connected with *bodies*: *sky* blue, *lavender*
blue, *turquoise* blue, *gentian* blue, *violet* blue, *cornflower* blue, *reed*
green, *apple* green, *olive* green, *almond* green, *sea* green, *emerald*
green…" What does she mean, "not by chance"? She points out
that each name associates a color with a texture: "transparent or
opaque, smooth, rough, dense, or friable bodies that shine, sparkle,
reflect, or shimmer softly or harshly in the light."

Then there are the name choices for what are generally thought
of as the first synthetic, meaning aniline, dyes discovered in the
mid-nineteenth century, the best known of which is *mauve*, the

French name of the common mallow plant; the crimson red named *fuchsin* after the fuchsia; and then that cross between mauve and fuchsin known as *dahlia*, soon followed by *Britannia violets*.

Such names are fake, allusions to what paints used to be before the industrial production of paints with which light has an easier time than before—easier in the sense that light is not whacked around as it might be with its passage through a series of differently shaped crystals, as in the case of lapis lazuli or, for that matter, in the case of the colors of the sky in storms or at dawn and sunset, when we suddenly sit up and see the color as if for the first time.

The fakeness of these bodies conjured by market hype is a fakeness brought about because the body was killed off by mid-nineteenth century. What took its place were these names as substitutes for what had gone, and the names were marvelous. Of course, the broad strokes of the colors of nature remain accessible to human experience in the seas, the skies, the plowed fields and forests, in the human face and body, no less than in the flash of fur and wing of animals and birds, not to mention the rusted edges of shop awnings and the mold in the bathroom.

Yet the very same chemical revolution of the nineteenth century that emerged from the search for color and drugs from coal tar, this very same chemical revolution polluted those broad strokes of remaining nature with new texture. The sunsets never looked so stunning as they did through the haze of factory smoke and soot. Surrealism arrived long before the Surrealists caught on. The moon radiated chemical purple, streams ran with phosphorescent blue or thick green sludge. A stench and pall clung to the air. Small wonder the upper classes of England and Germany sought the beauty of the natural colors of Italy and the south of France, and raved about the "quality of the light" that hung like wings of gossamer over silky sunsets. And of course these purple moons and phosphorescent streams back home in the industrial north appeared all the more vivid on account of the dull, bleak carapace that coated everything else, including the human lung. Iron and coal dominated this period.

"Their colour spread everywhere," writes Lewis Mumford, "from grey to black: the black boots, the black stove-pipe hat, the black coach or carriage, the black iron frame of the hearth, the black cooking pots and pans and stove. Was it protective coloration? Was it mere depression of the senses?"[8]

Thanks to the chemical revolution wrought from coal, we now live in an artificial world without much awareness as to its artificiality. Most everything around us derives from coal chemistry, and this applies especially to the way we have recast the color of the world such that we have confused the factory-made color world around us in our rooms and magazines, our clothing and automobiles, with the colors in nature, parallel to the way we have confused a photograph with reality.

The fake names of synthetic colors do more than what Anita Albus points to. These names take all that color has been with reference to the world of plants, bugs, and minerals, and adds the magic of artifice, frequently the colonial exotic—as when Roland Barthes notes in his quirky autobiography, first published in 1975, that when he buys colors he does so according to "the mere sight of their name." What he says is: "The name of the color (*Indian yellow*, *Persian red*, *celadon green*) outlines a kind of generic region within which the exact, special effect of the color is unforeseeable; the name is then the promise of a pleasure, the program of an operation."[9]

Barthes recruits the special but unforeseeable effect of these largely colonial color names to destabilize the very idea of a code, in the same way that Joseph Conrad, in *Heart of Darkness* (1899), flits between the solid colors of the map of Africa and the evanescent colors of the flames racing across the water of the Thames in the rays of the setting sun when his narrator, a simple sailor by the name of Marlow, gives voice to his soul-cracking experience in the Congo with the curious statement, *the fascination of the abomination*. Barthes uses the solidity of the colonial category—for example, *Indian yellow*—to shake things up back home by the Seine, a task made easy by the mystery of India, let us say, making for an elegant play of the fixed and the elusive. A great student of reading and writing, film and photography, Barthes himself loved to paint and is credited with over seven hundred drawings and paintings, the few I have seen being spidery meanderings of dots and lines hell-bent on evading the code, not unlike the work of Cy Twombly. Being unforeseeable introduces into color the element of chance, where the "color walks" of William S. Burroughs become evidence of color's ability to itself walk. As Barthes says, the name of the color transports him.

And not only Barthes or Burroughs, but Goethe as well strikes an equally color-active tone when he cites Philipp Otto Runge on account of his focus on transparent colors as polymorphous magical substances that lead a life of their own, spiraling off into nether regions of soul and mind. With transparent color, "objects are cloaked with a charm," Runge writes, "that usually lies more in the air lying between us and the object than in the lighting of its forms."[10]

This reminds me of magic lanterns and the translucent colors they projected, filling the air with shimmering color. Recorded as early as 1646, such machines found color-magic a congenial helpmate for their spectacular displays, effortlessly transmuting the color on the glass slide or mirror into transparent color. Thus magic lanterns filled the centuries between Gothic stained glass and modern cinema. In my version of color history, magic lanterns took up where van Eyck (1390–1441) and Vermeer (1632–75) left off. The nineteenth century may have killed off the body of color, but in doing so it resurrected its spirit with the improvements made to long-existing machines that projected light through colored images, thereby entering into that same ethereal region, that "generic region," that Roland Barthes sees whenever he goes to buy a color and does so according to the *sight* of its *name* … think India, think Persia.

This connection between the body and soul of color by means of language was seen clearly by Marcel Proust, who frequently claims that Vermeer's painting provided him with his philosophy of writing. It is an amazing assertion: *style is to the writer what color is to the painter*, Proust's insistent point being that this art, working through layers of color and light, achieves its revelatory power through indirection and never by means of conscious confrontation, because the real treasure is inaccessible to the intellect.[11]

As a child, Proust's narrator was given a magic lantern by his parents. It would be set up on top of his lamp before the dinner hour and, "after the fashion of the first architects and glaziers of the Gothic age, it replaced the opacity of the walls with impalpable iridescences, supernatural multicolored apparitions, where legends were depicted as in a wavering, momentary stained-glass window."[12]

Proust's style is itself a magic lantern (the title of Howard Moss's marvelous book on Proust), which, in its most concentrated form, is what springs into being with the famous *memoire involontaire*, the fire ignited by the play of transparent colors with opaque ones. Runge talked of rebirth along with vanishing when he tried to put words to transparent color. This rebirth is as much memory as color, memories that can never be accessed by conscious effort no matter how hard we try, as when Proust's narrator imagines real persons as characters in the stained-glass window of the local church, made not just of color but of changing color, like Gilbert the Bad changing from cabbage green to plum blue, or like the persons in his magic-lantern show bathed continuously in a sunset of orange light.[13]

Slides and cinema project the spirit of color's dying corpse, as when the glittering firmament of lapis lazuli slides off the painter's palette, to be reborn in colored air of magical polymorphous substance. Slides and cinematic images seem to have depth as well. It is this mix of depth and transparency that allows them to bathe us in sunsets of orange as we sit in the darkness of theaters, washed by color and the crunching of popcorn.

1. Martin Gusinde, *Los indios de Tierra del Fuego*, vol.1, *Los Selk'nam*, trans. Werner Hoffmann (Buenos Aires: Centro Argentino de Etnología Américana, 1982), 716–18.
2. E. Lucas Bridges, *Uttermost Part of the Earth* (London: Hodder and Stoughton, 1951), 716–18.
3. Anita Albus, *The Art of Arts: Rediscovering Painting* (New York: Knopf, 2000), 67.
4. Ibid., 93.
5. Ibid., 65.
6. Jane Alison, "Colour Me In," in *Colour after Klein: Re-Thinking Colour in Modern and Contemporary Art* (London: Black Dog Publishing, 2005), 15.
7. François Delamare and Bernard Guineau, *Colors: The Story of Dyes and Pigments* (New York: Harry N. Abrams, 2000), 125. Delamare was director of research at the Écoles des Mines, Paris, studying Roman and Gallic-Roman pigments as well as modern industrial paints. A physicist and research engineer, Guineau has worked with historians on the history of pigments and has written a book on pigments and dyes from antiquity to the Middle Ages.
8. Lewis Mumford, *Technics and Civilization* (New York: Harcourt Brace, 1963 [1934]), 163.
9. Roland Barthes, *Roland Barthes by Roland Barthes*, trans. Richard Howard (New York: Farrar, Straus and Giroux, 1977 [1975]), 129. Many thanks to Brigit Potter for showing me this.
10. Philipp Otto Runge, letter to Goethe, July 5, 1806, reproduced in full in Albus, *Art of Arts*, 80. This letter was omitted from the English translation of Goethe's color book, which was, in my opinion, a huge mistake.
11. Marcel Proust, *In Search of Lost Time*, vol. 6, *Time Regained*, trans. Andreas Mayor and Terence Kilmartin, revised by D.J. Enright (New York: Modern Library, 1993), 299.
12. Proust, *In Search of Lost Time*, vol. 1, *Swann's Way*, trans. Lydia Davis (New York: Viking, 2003), 9.
13. Ibid., 175.

Conversation with Aslı Çavuşoğlu

—

Natalie Bell

Natalie Bell: One of the themes I see frequently in your work is forensics and its relationship to archaeology, but also its connection to interpretation and how we think about art objects, whether contemporary or historical. I'm curious how you approach the idea of forensics or the interpretation of objects or a crime scene, as in *Murder in Three Acts* (2012), which is also about art objects, albeit in a different narrative language. How do you think about an object's afterlife by way of interpretation?

Aslı Çavuşoğlu: Actually, archaeology and forensics are more modus operandi for me than the themes of my work. I am comfortable within these fields because they can be analogies for many things: How do we create stories, fictions, and/or national narratives through objects? Or, how do we extract the true value of art objects? How do we make connections? How do we project ourselves onto objects such that our ideas redefine them? I'm more interested in that process than in archeology itself.

NB: That seemed to be what was at work in "The Stones Talk," your solo show at ARTER (2013), in which you recreated fragmented bits of archaeological finds, or "study pieces," that are considered too partial for museum display. I wonder if some part of that had to do with thinking about the fragments per se, and what it means to have something irreparably partial, in terms of how we approach its value and use.

AÇ: I heard from an archaeologist who was working in Çatalhöyük, an archaeological site in Turkey, who told me about an early excavation in that area in which they excavated a female idol lacking a head; the archaeologists of the time thought that it would be ugly to show it that way, so they made a head for her. But they used materials and techniques to integrate a head that a viewer wouldn't understand to be added later. It got me thinking about who decides what is lacking or inconsequential, or how this manipulation of archaeological objects can alter the story they offer, and how, with display and its hierarchies, museums help to create nationalism, to make the viewer conform to an identity.

I was thinking about how other narratives can be employed or how other display methods can change the story these objects are telling. The name of the exhibition is paraphrased from Freud, actually. Freud was using all these archaeological objects, small idols, showing them to his patients and asking them to interpret them, and there, of course, they were not in a museum. They were just on his desk. So then, he writes this very beautiful lecture, "The Aetiology of Hysteria" (1896), which he concludes with a Latin phrase, "Saxa loquuntur!": *Stones speak*. He says that it's never the object speaking. It's our ideas, and we make them speak.

NB: Many of your projects consider the way cultural heritage is constructed. Sometimes that happens through archaeology, sometimes through a particular landscape or site, and sometimes by calling upon a specific figure, such as Alexander the Great. How did that inquiry first emerge in your work, and where does it stand in your thinking at this point?

AÇ: One of my early projects was titled *The Demolition of the Russian Monument at Ayestefanos* (2011). Its long title comes from the first Turkish-made film in history. The history of Turkish cinema starts with this film, but nobody saw it, so nobody knows if it existed or not. After the Turkish Republic was formed, the government was trying to find the first Turkish somethings—first Turkish painter, first Turkish filmmaker, and so on. They completely ignored all the heritage of the Ottomans, so they were trying to find Turk-Turk filmmakers, not Greek-Turk. The Manaki brothers, the second filmmakers in the world, after the Lumière brothers, were from Albania—born into a Greek family, but just happened to die in a place that now belongs to Macedonia. However, they were left out of Turkish film history and a ghost film was nominated as the first.

The Alexander the Great statue I made [*Gordian Knot* (2013)] was about the debate between Macedonia and Greece: both countries were saying, "He's *our* hero, so he cannot be *yours*." It lasted maybe fifteen years. Recently they agreed that Macedonia would change its name. Macedonia is now called North Macedonia because of this dispute.

NB: I had no idea it was about something so ancient.

AÇ: Especially after the collapse of the Soviet Union, every Balkan country was trying to find some basis to claim that it should be a separate country, so they had to come up with historical figures and stories. This selection of the figureheads or pioneers of a culture, tied to ethnic background or country, is something I find very primitive, yet effective. I am curious how the Manaki brothers or Alexander the Great would relate themselves to the Balkans now.

I find UNESCO and its claims about cultural heritage problematic as well. They say, "Culture is for everybody," but if you don't have a visa, if you can't afford international travel, you can't visit UNESCO sites. It's not for everyone, actually, if we are honest about political and economic realities. We can see the problem with Syrian heritage and who is claiming it now. All these 3-D printers are making copies of Palmyra, and I'm wondering who has the copyright and to what end could it be reproduced? To place a replica of one of the main arches of Palmyra in London, in Trafalgar Square,[1] is completely kidnapping, hijacking Syrian cultural heritage, and claiming that it all gained relevance to the Western world primarily because it was a Roman site, a "desired" past of Europe.

NB: Cultural heritage, and how it can be read into the landscape, also informs your project for Manifesta 11, with the thrift-store landscape paintings you found and manipulated [*Muthoscapes* (2016)].

AÇ: I really like the word pentimento; that's what the work is about. It's an Italian word to describe when a painter changes his or her idea and repaints the painting. The term relates to regret, and also nostalgia. My aim was to collect landscape paintings of Switzerland and find the very first brushstrokes of all these anonymous painters who, when they painted the mountains, changed their minds and placed them somewhere else. I tried to create a metaphor for a utopian place that's just on the axis in the very first layer, that is now completely erased by another landscape painting.

NB: Do they usually start with the mountain?

AÇ: Yes. They start in the center with the biggest mountains. Of course, I cannot detect which mountain was painted first, but at least I can tell that they changed and erased some parts and painted over them. My idea was to make the covered-up mountains emerge again, also in relation to the idea of Switzerland as a haven or utopia, a branding strategy employed especially after the Second World War. In fact, it is the most difficult country to immigrate to.

NB: Many of your other works are also about uncovering things that are hidden, whether literally or figuratively, and particularly about historical moments or aspects of a political history that have not been publicly recognized or sufficiently acknowledged. What about your short film *In Different Estimations Little Moscow* (2011), in which you looked at a very specific historical event in Turkey—the 1980 coup d'état trial, known as Point Operation, in which the government prosecuted those involved in a short-lived democratic movement in Fatsa—but uncovered it through different personal recollections? It seems like for many people, this history still felt unsafe.

AÇ: The work reflects upon personal stories that are inconsistent with each other, because the story of the 1980 coup in Fatsa was never allowed to be written. What happened there was never told; it was never recorded or publicly discussed. Even the families from there never told their children what happened.

NB: How much of that project was improvised along the way?

AÇ: Actually, I had no idea what I would find when I first embarked on that project, so I wanted to go to Fatsa first to get a sense of the atmosphere. I thought reenactment wouldn't be a good idea because I wouldn't want to evoke a trauma if people were still hurt by past events. I was trying to be respectful of their memories. I just wanted to hear what people would say about this event, if they wanted to speak about it at all; what I heard were all the scattered histories about what happened—inconsistent places, people, incidents, shootings, etc. I was thinking the core idea would be to reflect this fragmentation, that there's no one linear history about the military operation. Nobody agrees with each other, and some people haven't spoken to each other in forty years and they have completely different things to say. Especially because talking about this incident was banned. I thought my approach would be more artistic and more ethical if I just made space for all the stigmatized stories and showed that it's impossible to place all these small pieces to create something linear.

NB: What was your experience working on *The Cut* (2015)? How did people perceive that project in Warsaw, and what was the reaction or expectation from the community when they saw their landscape excavated to reveal these World War II–era ruins?

AÇ: We received, of course, very diverse responses, but I remember one opposing view. There was this neighbor who said, "I want to forget. Why do you make me remember?" He meant, "I know that we live in ruins, and there are so many dead people underneath the earth, but I cannot continue if I know it all the time." He was right. It was a nice trigger to start a conversation with different people, because others had said they were happy to see the rubble of the ghetto, so all these horrible things wouldn't happen again. That's why we wanted to make it only a three-day event that would unearth a terrifying past and leave it to be covered by oblivion again. We made a cut, or an excavation, and then together we filled the earth with all these materials we extracted, not making any hierarchical order and not valuing one over another, and just put the grass on top of it to mark that it was discovered and could be interpreted and excavated again. I think this is what I am trying to do in most of my projects. I'm not trying to say this is the right version of the story, or this is the right way to look at or interpret things. It's more an attempt to open up to multiplying narratives. You can have your own interpretation. Narratives are all constructed, so they can be reconstructed again and again.

NB: Another work that takes up history and censorship is *191/205* (2010), in which you look back at words that were banned by Turkish state media. What's surprising for me about those words is that many are themselves about memory and history. Could you discuss how you first learned about that list of words and how you developed the piece?

AÇ: Actually, when I was pursuing the list of these banned words, I was so sure that those times of censorship had passed and that it would never be like that again. I had, I guess, a nostalgic view of this past military coup and censorship issues, because it was 2010— which is not that long ago—and we had a really great, free life in Istanbul. For my friends, my generation, when I first talked about the project, they were like, "Oh, that's absurd! Did it really happen?" In fact, two years after I made the project, there was an internet ban. Some words were banned in domain names, together with some blogs and some online news sites. There was a really big protest about it.

The use of language has been very definitive; especially then, leftists and rightists had quite particular and divided jargons. For instance, one would say "entire," the other would say "whole." And through these uses of words you could tell people's political inclinations. The polarization of everyday language continues even now. If somebody passes away, there are two ways to offer condolences: one is a new one, made up by secularists, and the other is more religious-sounding, more traditional.

NB: Can you give an example from the banned list?

AÇ: They were saying that you could not say "revolution," because it is very leftist, but we could say "reform," which is not exactly the same word. Or, instead of "equality," they were suggesting the Ottomanic version of the word that nobody uses, which has a lot of connotations of a glorified past. I had no idea what I was going to do with the list when I first pursued it. It took me six months to find the entire list.

NB: How did you go about compiling the complete list?

AÇ: I went to the archives of the state television and radio and they told me they have the right to burn down their archive every ten years—which is what they did, because what you choose to keep can be dangerous for the former director. So they burned it down, and it was only through the former director of the archive, who'd made a copy of this list for himself, that I got it. He sent me a photocopy of his own copy, which was a very bad photocopy: one page was almost completely black, you could hardly read the words, and there was one page missing. That's why the work is called "191 out of 205," because the remaining words were on that one page I was never able to find. I had this information and it didn't make sense to just put it on the walls, so I approached a Turkish-German rapper and he composed a song using all the words. It's a protest song about gentrification, corruption, many different political things, and it uses 191 of these words as well.

NB: Thinking about what can or can't be spoken, or the way censorship has manifested in present-day Turkey, leads me to a more recent work, *Future Tense* (2017), that concerns a moment in which censorship has taken an unusual direction.

AÇ: I can't recall his name, but there's a thinker from the Middle East who says, "If there's a government that's afraid of words, that means that words can still change things." Each time there is another wave of censorship, it proves that we should be hopeful that language and words are capable of change. *Future Tense* came out of a moment when a lot of journalists were jailed after the failed military coup in 2016, and all the commentators and journalists I find important to read were suddenly absent.

In all this turmoil, people were talking to each other and asking what would happen in the future. It occurred to me that astrologists and tarot card readers were playing a big part in the news and political commentary, even on TV, talking about what's going to happen next. I realized why they were so interesting to viewers—because this was also what normal people, including the government, were doing: filling the gaps with gossip. The soothsayers would say whatever they wanted about politics; they were immune to censorship because they were using the tools of astrology and other supernatural elements.

There are very biased astrologists working in different newspapers, some pro-government, some anti-government. The astrological charts they publish in the papers are so political! And their interpretations reflect the politics of the newspaper they're working with. Ten years ago, when you would buy a newspaper, you were able to read different opinions. But nowadays it's one single opinion. There's no discussion, no opposing views. For *Future Tense*, I was wondering if it would be possible to have a newspaper in which I could invite all these different groups, different astrologists, so they could create a newspaper that is polyvocal. I invited about fifty soothsayers from Turkey, of diverse ethnicities and political orientations, to contribute. There are so many opposing views about the future of Turkey: one soothsayer says it's going to be divided; the other says it's going to be perfect, it's going to be bigger, like old times. So it's actually all about these people's aspirations. It's analogous to archaeology and archaeological objects. You try to compile all these different objects, interpretations, and histories to support your idea. Of course, I'm not saying "astrology and archaeology" because my archaeologist friend would kill me: "Can you compare us with astrology?"

1. A twenty-foot marble replica of the Arch of Triumph in Palmyra, made from 3-D renderings, was unveiled in London's Trafalgar Square in 2016. The original arch was destroyed by Islamic State militants in late 2015. The project was an initiative of the University of Oxford, Harvard University, and Dubai's Museum of the Future, which came together to form the Institute for Digital Archaeology.

Entropology

—

Mariana Castillo Deball

In the suburbs of Geneva, there lived a woman who was a mineralo-
gist and would pay any price for a good specimen. One day, as she
was fishing in the river, something caught her net, and diving down
she brought up a stone about a foot in diameter, beautifully carved
on all sides to resemble clustering hills and peaks. She was quite
as pleased with this, as if she had found some precious stone; and
having had an elegant stand made for it, she set her prize upon the
table. Whenever it was about to rain, clouds, which from a distance
looked like new cotton wool, would come forth from each of the
holes or grottoes on the stone, and appear to close them up. That's
how she started her stone collection.

As part of her daily routine, she wakes up a couple of hours before
heading to work. She starts the day arranging her stone garden,
composed of hundreds of samples collected throughout the years.
The "weird rocks" or "strange stones," as she calls them, are
arranged in a structure mimetic to mountains on a smaller scale.
Her favorite samples, used for the peaks of the miniature mountains, are larger at the top than below, giving them the appearance
of being about to soar into the air. At the beginning, she collected
samples on field trips, but when she started working at the materials testing laboratory, she began to experiment and create her own
stones that could never have been found in nature. The petrified
field gives the impression of a lunar landscape.

She prepared her suitcase for the next five days, as she was attend-
ing a session in which the participants stay in a special section of the
campus, in order to avoid distraction and maintain the shape of what
the boss calls the collective cloud of thoughts. It was springtime, and
as she stepped out the door, in front of her stood an idyllic landscape.
It was hard to imagine that one hundred yards underneath this soil
was a circular tunnel, seventeen miles in circumference, a powerful
and complicated machine that would smash particles together at
super-fast speeds in a bid to unlock the secrets of the universe. One
of the radio spots broadcasted recently came to her mind: "The Large
Hadron Collider at CERN in Geneva switches on after twenty years
of preparation, generating, in a microscopic region where beams

of particles collide, a concentration of energy that has never been achieved before—a concentration that mimics, in microcosm, the conditions that prevailed in the universe immediately after the big bang."

She cycled toward the laboratory, passing the Einstein avenue, followed by the Bohr street and the Galileo Galilei road, as she did every day. CERN, the *world's largest particle physics laboratory*, is an almost-utopian village of four thousand physicists. She worked at the materials testing laboratory, but once a month she was appointed to attend the "invention sessions" created to make insights to come up with ideas, to solve fundamental questions. The meeting was held in a conference room: plasma TV screens on the walls, a long table furnished with bottles of diet soft drinks and big bowls of cashews. They were eight people in the meeting. The man next to her was lean and sleek, with closely cropped, fine black hair; he told her that once he spent twenty-two days walking across Texas with nothing but a bedroll, a flashlight, and a rifle—from Big Bend, in the west, to Houston, where he was going to deliver a paper at a biology conference. On the other side of the table, an imposing man with graying red hair attracted her attention. Three or four pens were crammed into his shirt pocket. The screen saver on his laptop was a picture of Stonehenge.

She had divergent feelings about these meetings. On one hand, she liked the brainstorm of ideas, a sort of shower of thoughts that would sometimes last up to five days. The sessions were so intense that sometimes they continued discussing during the breaks and lunch hours. Every conversation was recorded and an attorney filled up files with the important ideas. The competition was quite hard, as everyone tried to express his or her brilliant thoughts, and this frequently made her tired; at some moments, she would just switch off from the meeting for a while. In order to maintain her thoughts elsewhere, she used to repeat in silence, word by word, a story that her grandmother used to tell her when she was a child:

> There was a town. There was a newly married youth.
> He went hunting. The newly married youth was a skillful

hunter. (I do not know his name.) He killed a mountain sheep. He skinned it. After skinning it, he felt hungry. He thought: "I will dry some of it, so that it may be light. I will carry it tomorrow. It is far, and it would be heavy if I should not dry it." Then he made a place to dry it. He began to cut up the meat, and hung it up. He was about to hang almost all of it on his drying frame. There were two thin pieces of meat lying there. He did not know where they fell off from. He was hungry. He thought: "I'll eat it." He put the meat on the fire, and when it was done, he ate. It tasted good. What he had killed did not taste that way. He thought: "What may it be that tastes so good?" He looked, and he saw that his own flesh was missing. He looked at it and saw that a knife had done it. Then he knew that it was his own flesh that tasted good. He thought: "Well, I'll cut off another piece of my flesh." He cut it off, put it on the fire, and when it was done he ate it. Then he saw that it tasted good. He wanted some more. He began to cook his flesh on the fire, and although he had eaten, he wanted some more. Then there was no more flesh on his legs. It was late at night, and he was still eating his flesh. In the morning, he was still eating. He wanted more. He could not stop eating. It was evening again, and he had eaten all his flesh. He had gnawed it off and only bones remained. He ate his own eyes, and only the orbits remained. He even ate his own tongue. He ate his whole body. Only his intestines remained, lying there. His intestines remained, and his throat. It was that way; he did not eat his intestines and his stomach. Only his bones remained; and he did not eat his brains and his marrow, but there was no more flesh in his skull. He was sitting down. Then he would not look any more at the mountain sheep.

When the "invention sessions" started ten years ago, they thought that it would be great if they came up with a half-dozen good ideas, and they came up with hundreds, currently filing five hundred a year. The director was kind of smart: instead of having a fixed team working on the inventions department, he brought together different combinations of specialists each time, who would brainstorm about certain issues. The idea started after observing that many discoveries were made by different people at the same time. The phenomenon of simultaneous discovery, called "multiples," turns out to be extremely common. Newton and Leibniz both discovered calculus. Charles Darwin and Alfred Russel Wallace both discovered evolution. The law of conservation of energy was formulated four times independently of each other. There seem to have been at least six inventors of the thermometer and no less than nine claimants of the invention of the telescope. The number of multiples could mean only one thing: scientific discoveries must, in some sense, be inevitable. They must be in the air, products of the intellectual climate of a specific time and place. This transformed the romantic notion of the genius. A scientific genius is not a person who does what no one else can do; he or she is someone who does what it takes many others to do.

On this occasion, the meeting was on the technology of self-assembly. What if it was possible to break a complex piece of machinery into a thousand pieces and then, at some predetermined moment, have the machine put itself back together again? That had to be useful, but for what?

The session started with discussion of whether there could be a machine capable of replacing the poet and the author. The problem was not thinking of a machine capable merely of "assembly-line" literary production, which would already be mechanical in itself, but a writing machine that would bring to the page all those things that we are accustomed to consider as the most jealously guarded attributes of our psychological life, our daily experience, our unpredictable changes of mood and inner elations, despairs, and moments of illumination. What would be the style of a literary automaton? The man with the red hair believed that its true voca-tion would be classicism. On the contrary, she proposed that this machine would serve a typical human need: the production of dis-order. The true literature machine would be one that itself feels the need to produce disorder, as a reaction against its preceding pro-duction of order—a machine that will produce avant-garde work to free its circuits when they are choked for too long by the production of classicism, proposing new ways of writing, turning its own codes completely upside down.

The discussion moved away from the literary field, reflecting on the possibility that the human endeavor to change nature would end up in exact imitation of the rules and proceedings of nature—but what would be the difference? Would there be a point when it would be impossible to discern a human creation from nature? Well, maybe the main difference is the amount of rubble we produce. Somehow, nature is able to bring everything back into a certain cycle, but we just produce more and more rubble.

At this death-point in the discussion, they headed to lunch. After the pause, she began to read a short paper she had prepared for the session:

Moondust. "I wish I could send you some," says Apollo 17 astronaut Gene Cernan.

Just a thimbleful scooped fresh off the lunar surface. "It's amazing stuff."

Feel it—it's soft like snow, yet strangely abrasive.

Taste it—"not half bad," according to Apollo 16 astronaut John Young.

Sniff it—"it smells like spent gunpowder," says Cernan.

How do you sniff moondust? Every Apollo astronaut did it. They couldn't touch their noses to the lunar surface. But after every moonwalk, they would tramp the stuff back inside the lander. Moondust was incredibly clingy, sticking to boots, gloves, and other exposed surfaces.

Did moondust remain hidden in the most intricate corners

of the travelers and their objects, making its way clandestinely back to Earth? It's hard to guess, but it is known that during the six Apollo surface excursions, the astronauts collected 2,415 samples of moon rocks, which constitute the lunar arsenal on Earth. Lunar samples are considered a limited national resource and future heritage, and are released only for approved applications in research, education, and public display.

The severe regulations for the use and distribution of extraterrestrial samples are quite different from the destiny of the objects brought to space by humans. Instead of measuring progress through technological achievements, the scope of human development could be determined by observing how far human debris has reached.

The image of an astronaut walking in slow motion on the quiet, desolate tract of the lunar surface, while his footprint—with a different gravitational force, perhaps with a lighter impact—leaves its unique trace, is far away; the lunar landscape is no longer a deserted land. Throughout the different expeditions and scientific experiments, humans brought hundreds of artificial objects to the Moon's surface, including exploration vehicles, parts of rockets, and several commemorative or personal objects left there by astronauts.

Lunar debris is not the only trace of humans in space; space waste—objects created by humans that no longer serve any useful purpose, in orbit around Earth—consists of everything from entire spent rocket stages and defunct satellites to explosion fragments, paint flakes, dust and slag from solid rocket motors, deliberately inserted small needles, and other small particles.

The number of objects in orbit is so big that it has surpassed a critical spatial density, especially because objects in orbit collide with each other, creating even more debris. The image of hundreds of useless objects orbiting around the Earth tells us something about what finally and probably will remain from the human attempt to transform their surroundings and expand their horizon. Progress and civilization might not be so efficient; we are probably just reaching a degree zero, a moment when expectations are not comparable with possibilities. Nevertheless, we carry on.

French anthropologist Claude Lévi-Strauss defined himself as a traveler, an archaeologist in space, vainly trying to restore exoticism with the use of particles and fragments. Lévi-Strauss never went to the Moon, but throughout his exploration of human nature in remote parts of the world, we could see with his magnifying glass the human tendency to reach zero. Human knowledge attempts to divide and fragment reality in order to understand it; words, concepts, mentalities, and disciplines constantly collide with each other, creating smaller and smaller particles, like moondust.

For Lévi-Strauss, mankind has constantly opposed itself to universal decay. Man appears as a machine, maybe more perfected than others, working on disaggregating an original order to precipitate organized matter into inertia. From the time he started to breathe and feed himself until the invention of the first thermonuclear and atomic instruments, man has done nothing but happily dissociate millions of structures to reduce them to a state in which they are not susceptible to integration. Without doubt, he has built cities and cultivated fields, but when thinking about it, these achievements are machines destined to produce inertia with a rhythm and proportion infinitely more elevated than the organization they imply. So, civilization, taken as a whole, can be described as a very complex mechanism busy fabricating what scientists call entropy, which means inertia. Every word exchanged, every printed line, establishes communication between two people, equaling a level that was previously characterized by a more complex organization. For Lévi-Strauss, instead of "anthropology" we should write "entropology," a name for a discipline dedicated to studying this process of disintegration in its more complex manifestations.[1]

Entropology could be described as a fight against time, a battle that in some cases tries to stop it, accelerate it, or even reverse it. The ambition to go backward in time, to a moment before humans, the Earth, and even the universe existed, is represented clearly by the experiment that will be performed this summer in our laboratory, which is trying to answer the questions, what is the universe made of and how did it all begin?

"The Large Hadron Collider at CERN in Geneva switches on after twenty years of preparation, generating, in a microscopic region where beams of particles collide, a concentration of energy that has never been achieved before—a concentration that mimics, in microcosm, the conditions that prevailed in the universe during the first trillionth of a second after the big bang."

Could this experiment be defined as reverse engineering? Reverse engineering is often done because the documentation of a particular device has been lost (or was never written), and the person who built the device is no longer available. The difference is that the event to be recreated is the beginning of the universe.

The session was interrupted at this moment, and they decided to discuss the paper the following day. She walked to her temporary room next to the conference hall. She never understood why they were obliged to sleep at the institute after such meetings; she wondered if they were also recording her dreams.

Before going to sleep, she read the final part of the short story "The
Trouble with Bubbles," in which Philip K. Dick imagines a future
where mankind has attempted to reach other intelligent forms
through space exploration, and has found nothing. In light of this
yearning to connect with other life forms, people can buy a plastic
bubble known as Worldcraft, the tagline of which reads, "Own your
own world!" The owner of Worldcraft is able to create a whole universe, controlling all the variables. In the story, there is a contest to
create the best Worldcraft universe. People spend months and even
years perfecting their pocket-size universes. After a couple of years,
a strange habit starts to appear; the winner of the best Worldcraft,
after receiving the prize, would smash the bubble into pieces as a
sort of cathartic action, and afterwards, in the same manner, the rest
of the participants would follow:

> All around the room other owners were smashing their
> worlds, stepping on them, grinding the delicate control mech-
> anisms underfoot. Men and women in a frenzy of abandon,
> quivering in an orgy of Dionysian lust. Crushing and breaking
> their carefully constructed worlds, one after another…

> "The bubbles seemed like a good idea, at first. We couldn't
> leave Terra so we built our own worlds right here. Sub-
> atomic worlds, in controlled containers. We start life going
> on a sub-atomic world, feed it problems to make it evolve,
> try to raise it higher and higher. … It's certainly a creative
> pastime. Not a merely passive viewing like television. In
> fact, world-building is the ultimate art form. It takes the
> place of all entertainments, all the passive sports as well
> as music and painting—"

> But something went wrong…

> At first it was creative. Everybody bought a Worldcraft
> bubble and built his own world. Molded life. Controlled it.
> Competed with others to see who could achieve the most
> advanced world.

"And it solved another problem … [t]he problem of leisure. With robots to work for us and robants to serve us and take care of our needs—"

"Too much leisure. Nothing to do. That, and the disappointment of finding our planet the only habitable planet in the system. …"

"But why? … Sadism? No, not exactly. More a sort of curiosity. Power. Why does a child break things? Power, again. We must never forget something. … These worlds are like toy boats in a bath tub. Or model rocketships you see kids playing with. They're surrogates, not the actual thing."[2]

1. Claude-Lévi Strauss, *Tristes Tropiques* (Paris: Librairie Plon, 1955). Free translation by the author.
2. Philip K. Dick, "The Trouble with Bubbles," in *Second Variety: Collected Stories*, vol. 2 (London: Gollancz, 1987), 195–7.

The text includes modified quotes from the following sources:
Italo Calvino, "Cybernetics and Ghosts," in *The Literature Machine* (London: Secker and Warburg, 1987).
Alexander Francis Chamberlain and Franz Boas, *Kutenai Tales* (Washington, DC: Smithsonian Institution, Bureau of American Ethnology, 1918).
Malcolm Gladwell, "In the Air: Who says big ideas are rare?," *New Yorker*, May 12, 2008.

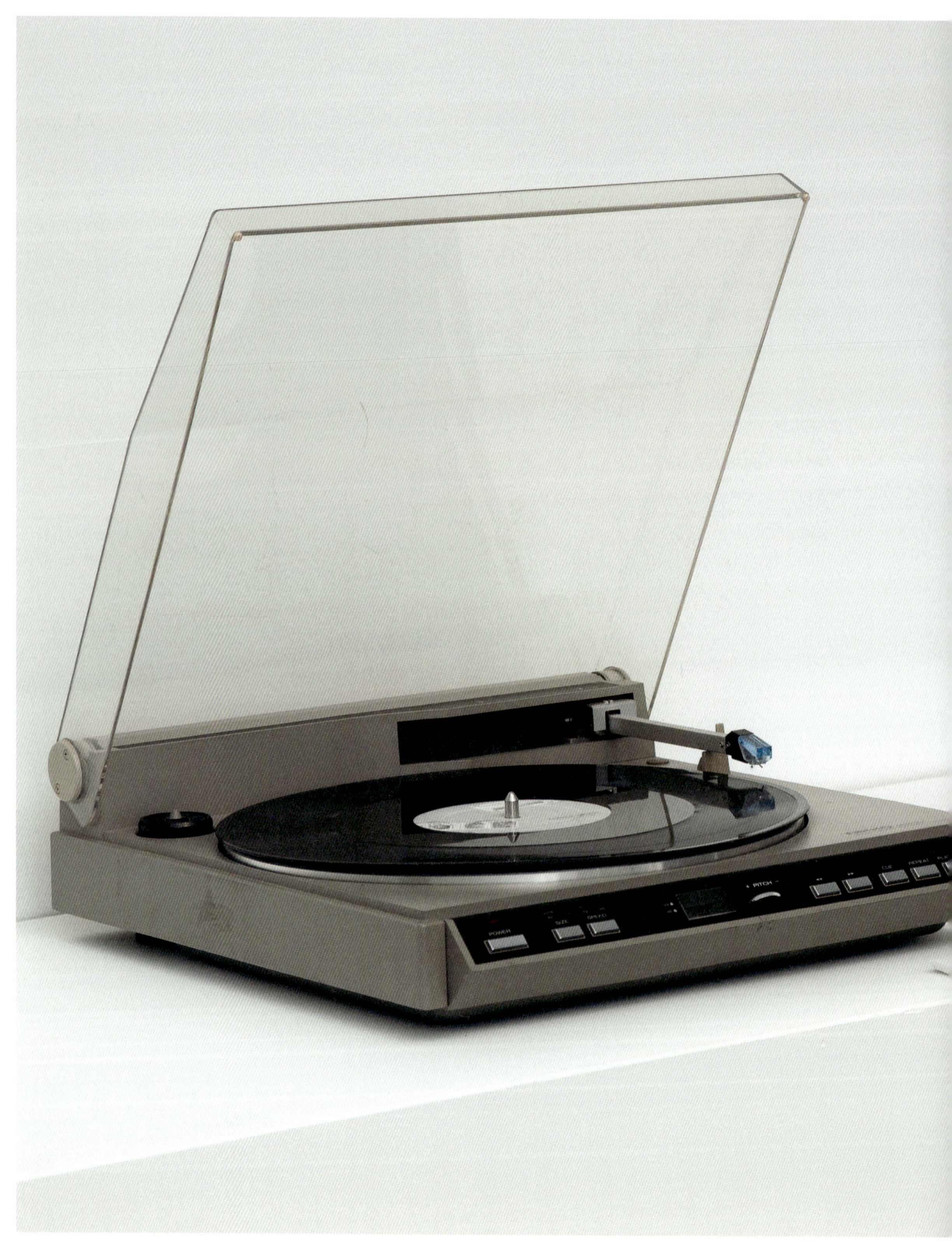

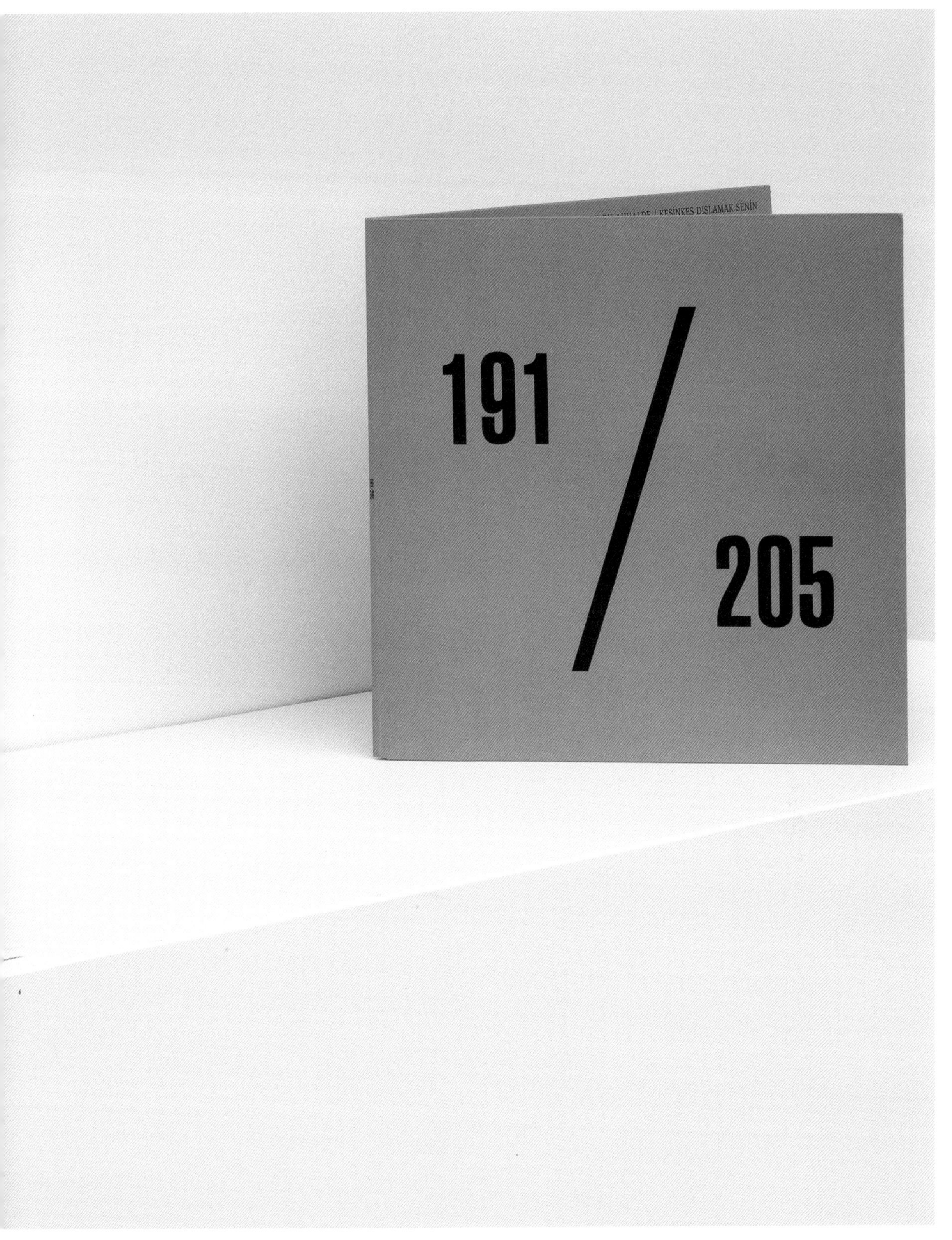

191 / 205
KESİNKES DİSLAMAK SENİN

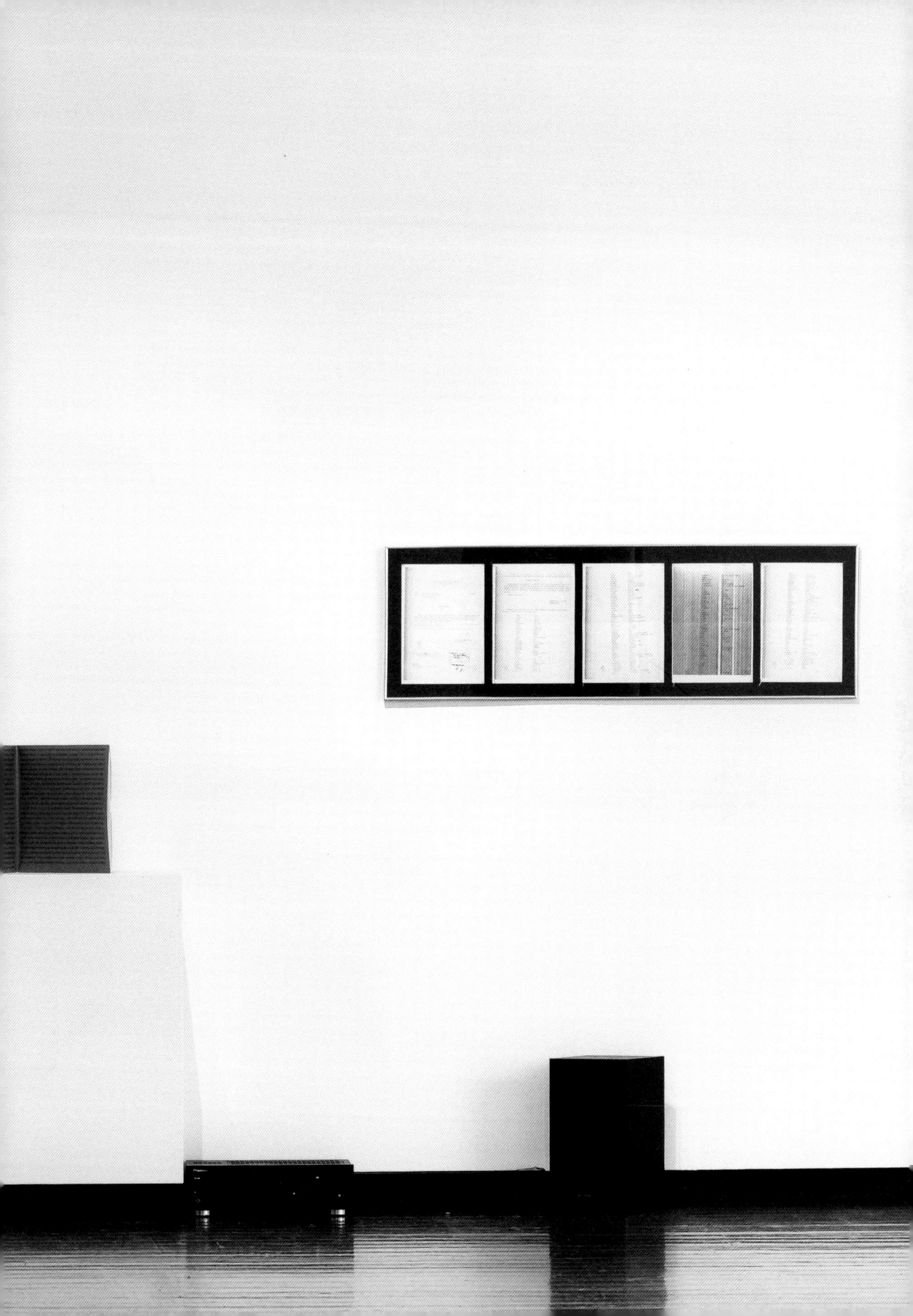

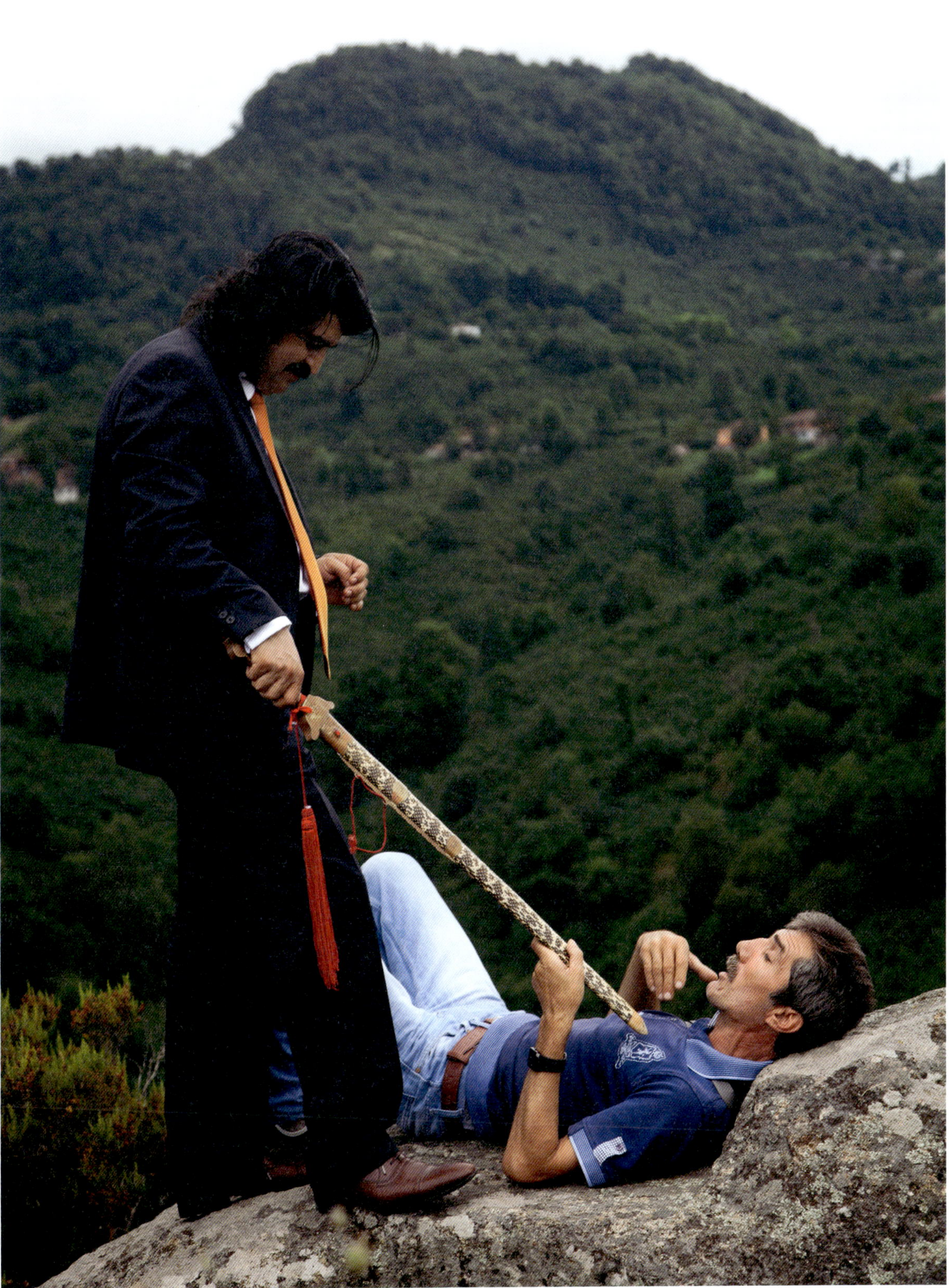

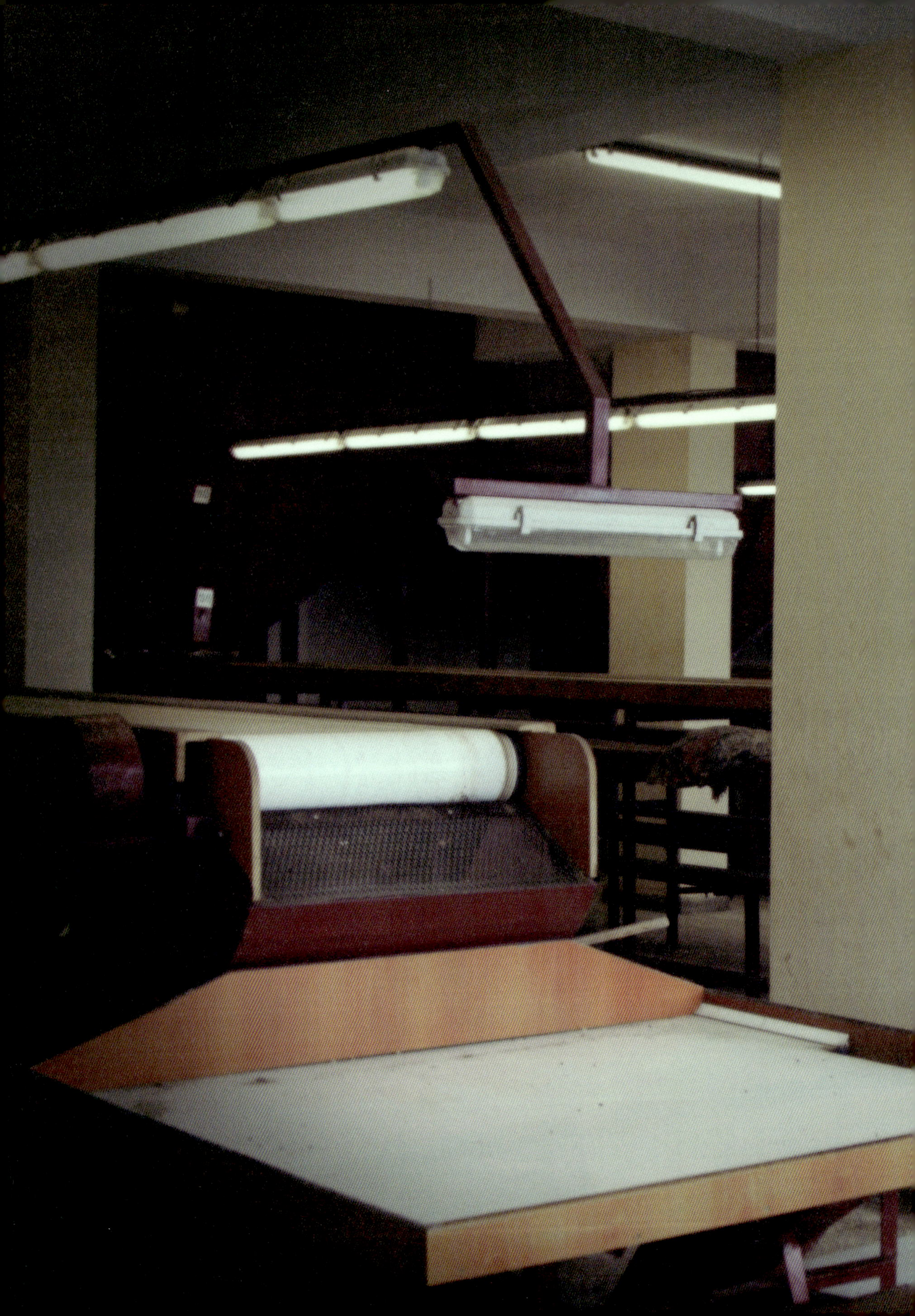

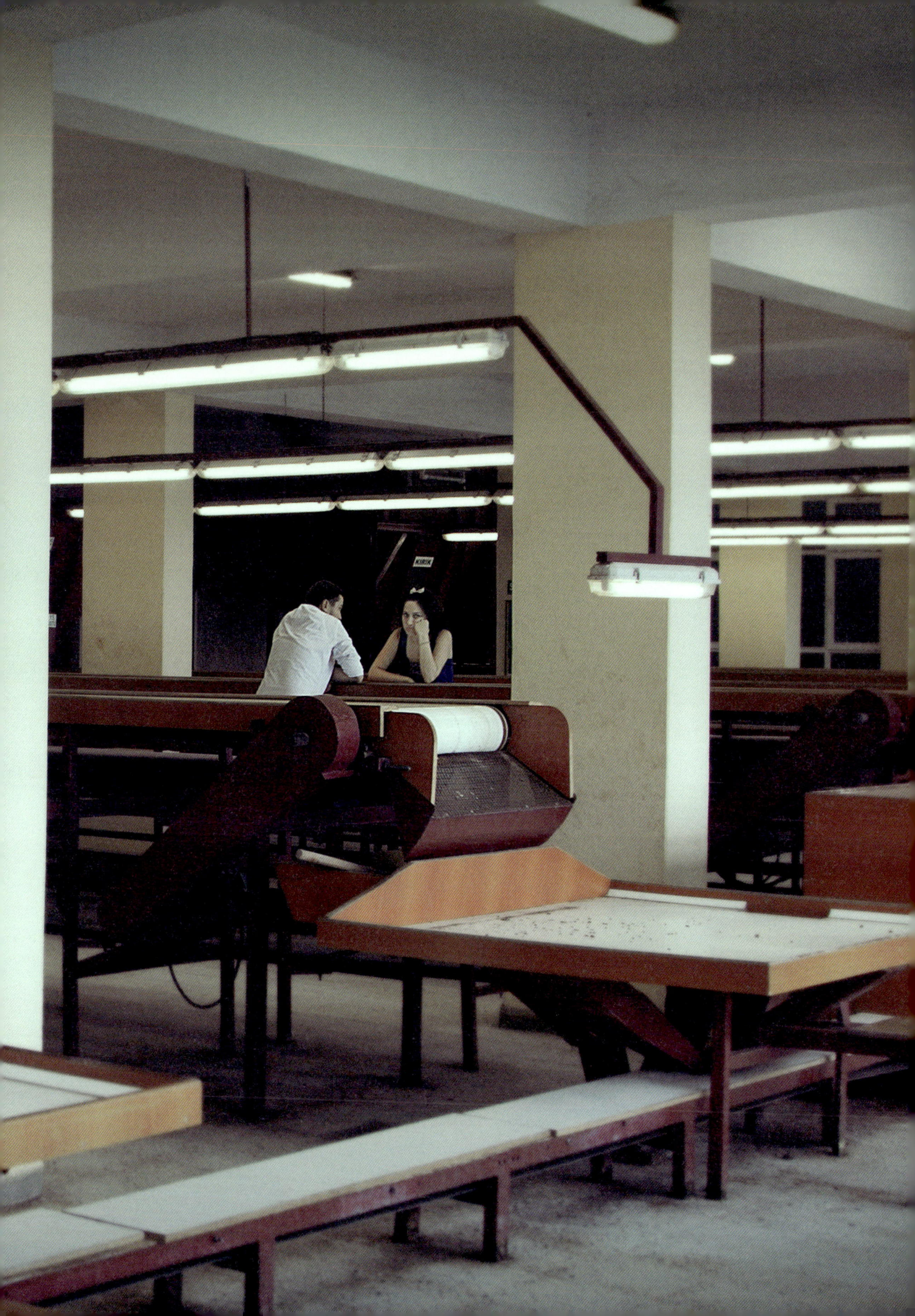

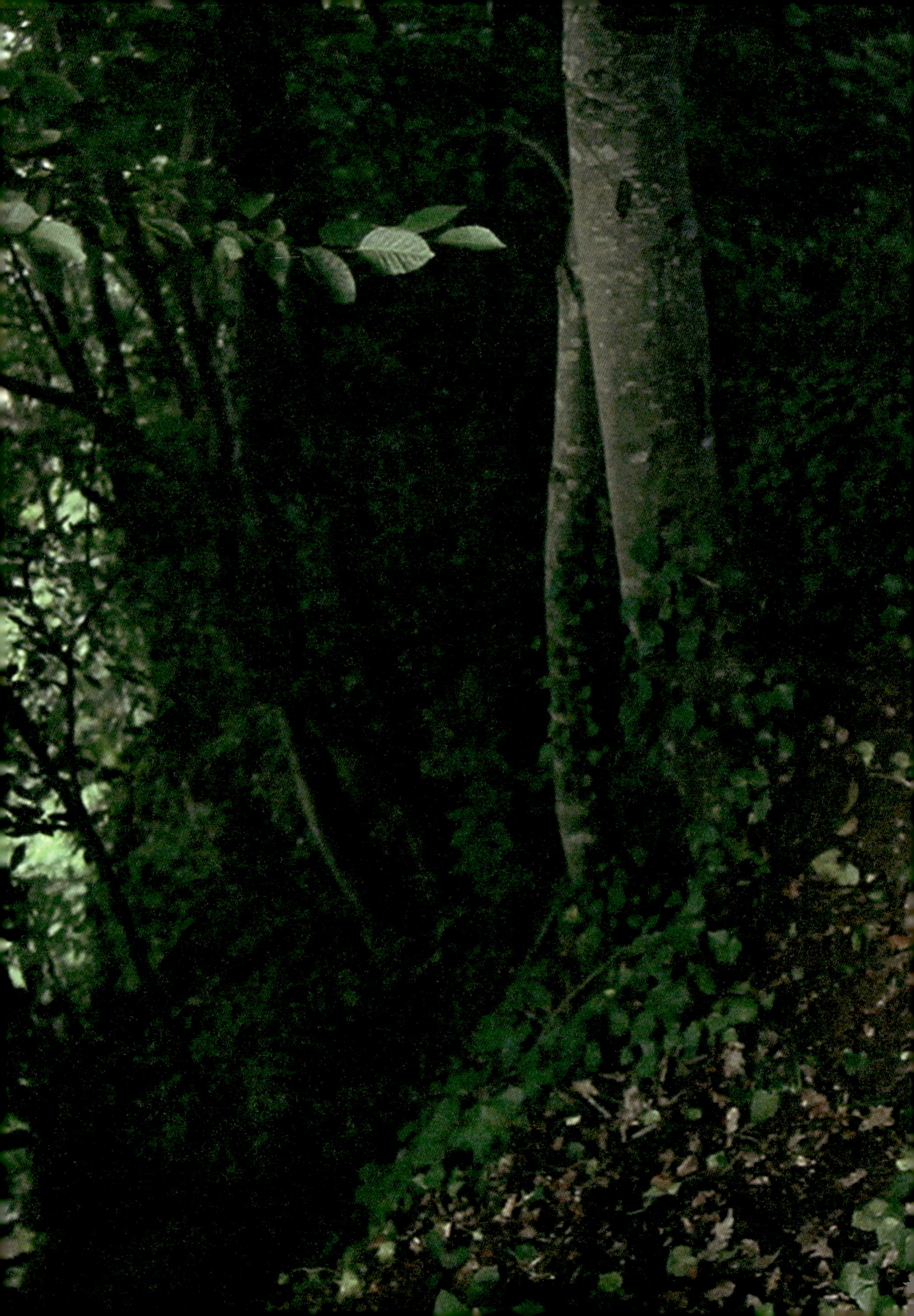

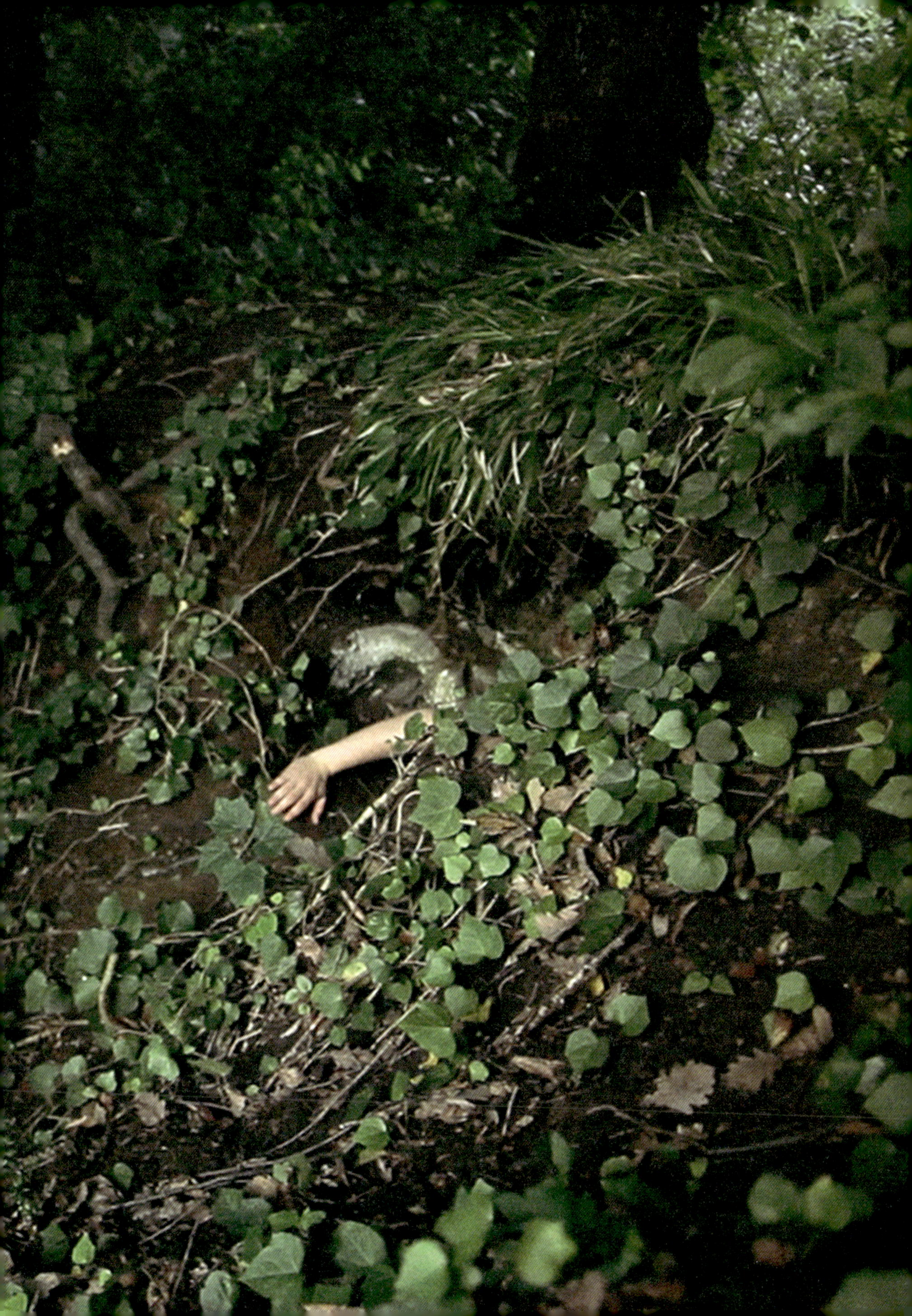

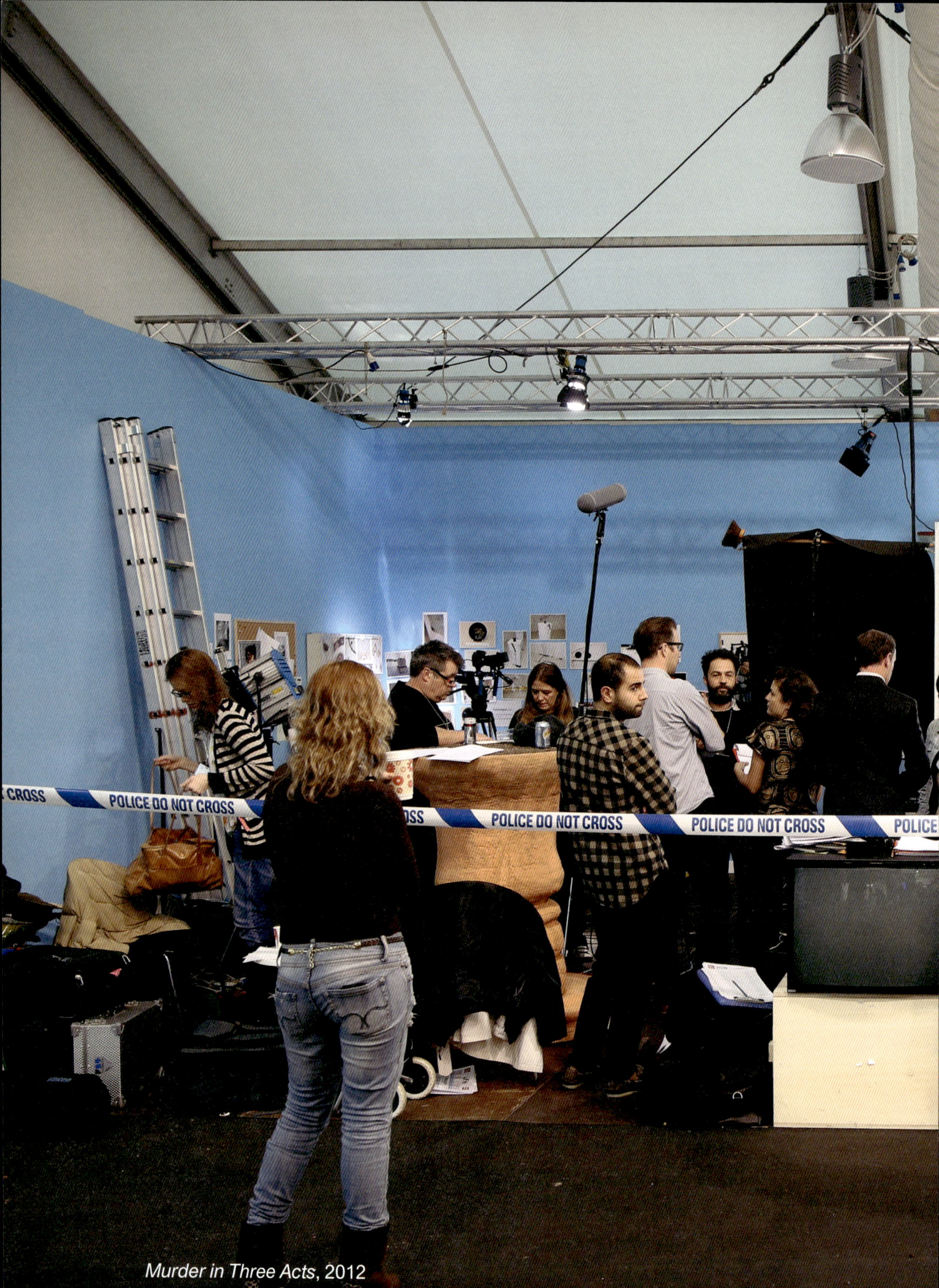

Murder in Three Acts, 2012

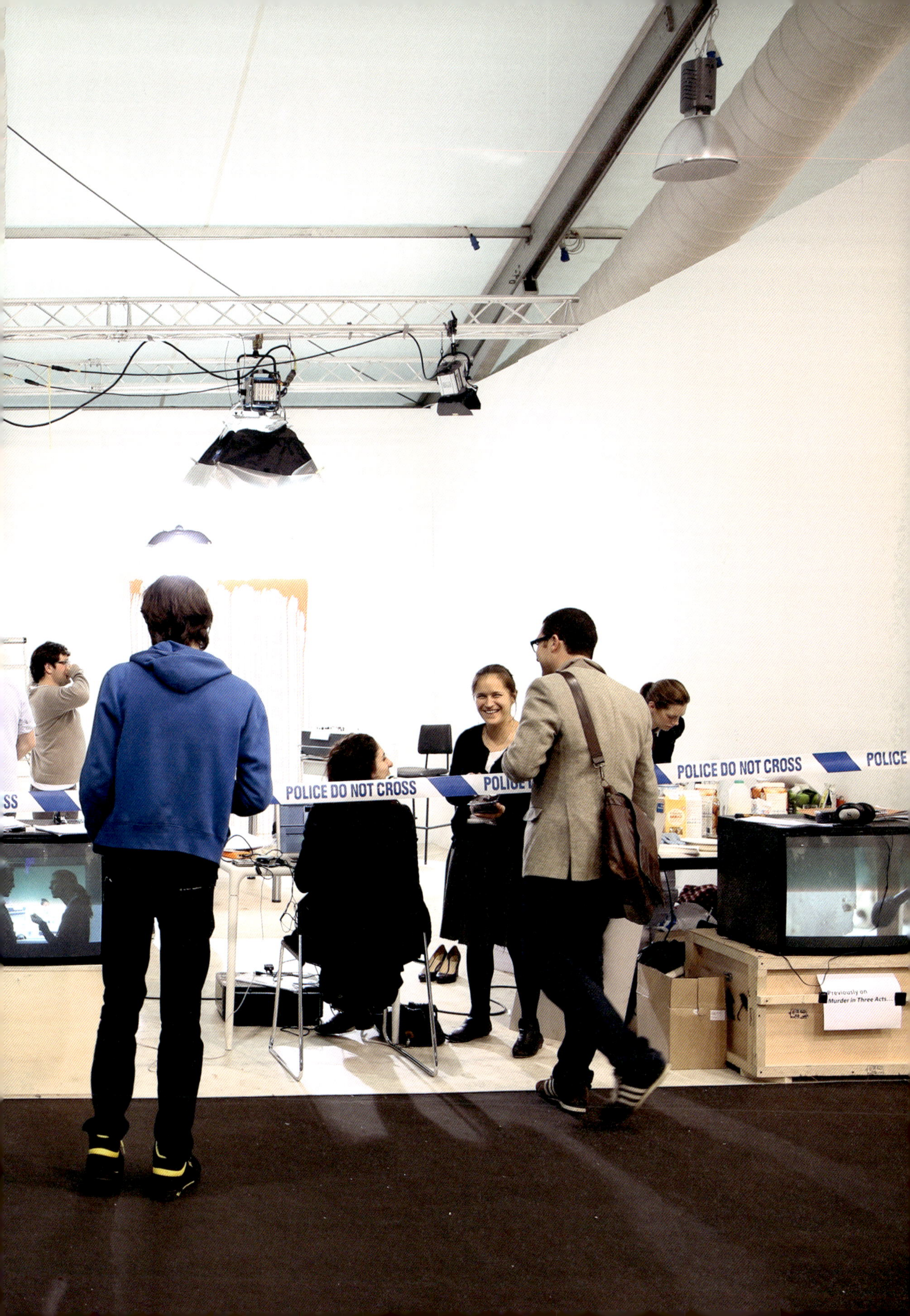

POLICE DO NOT CROSS
POLICE
POLICE DO NOT CROSS
POLICE
POLICE DO NOT CROSS
Previously on
Murder in Three Acts...

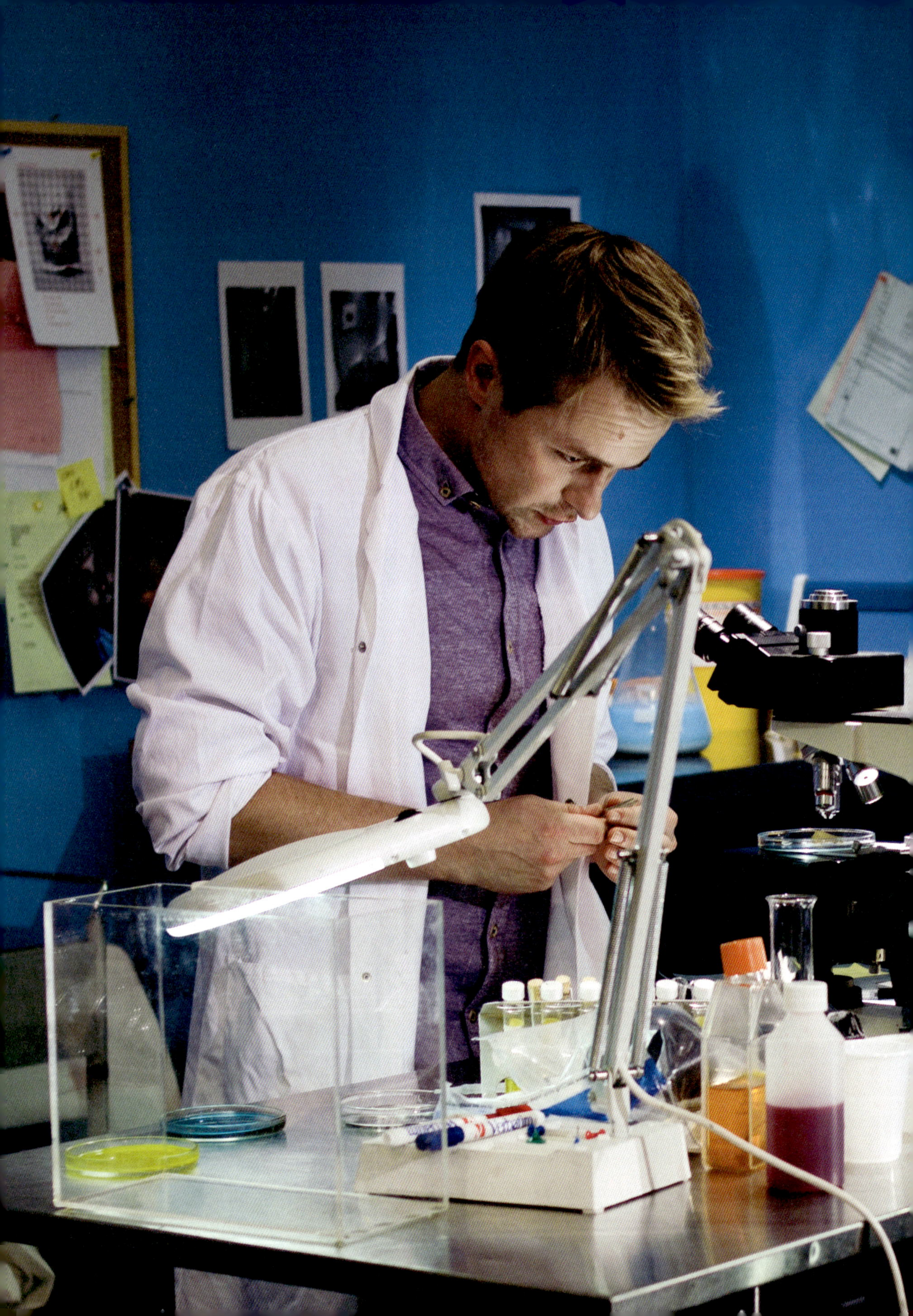

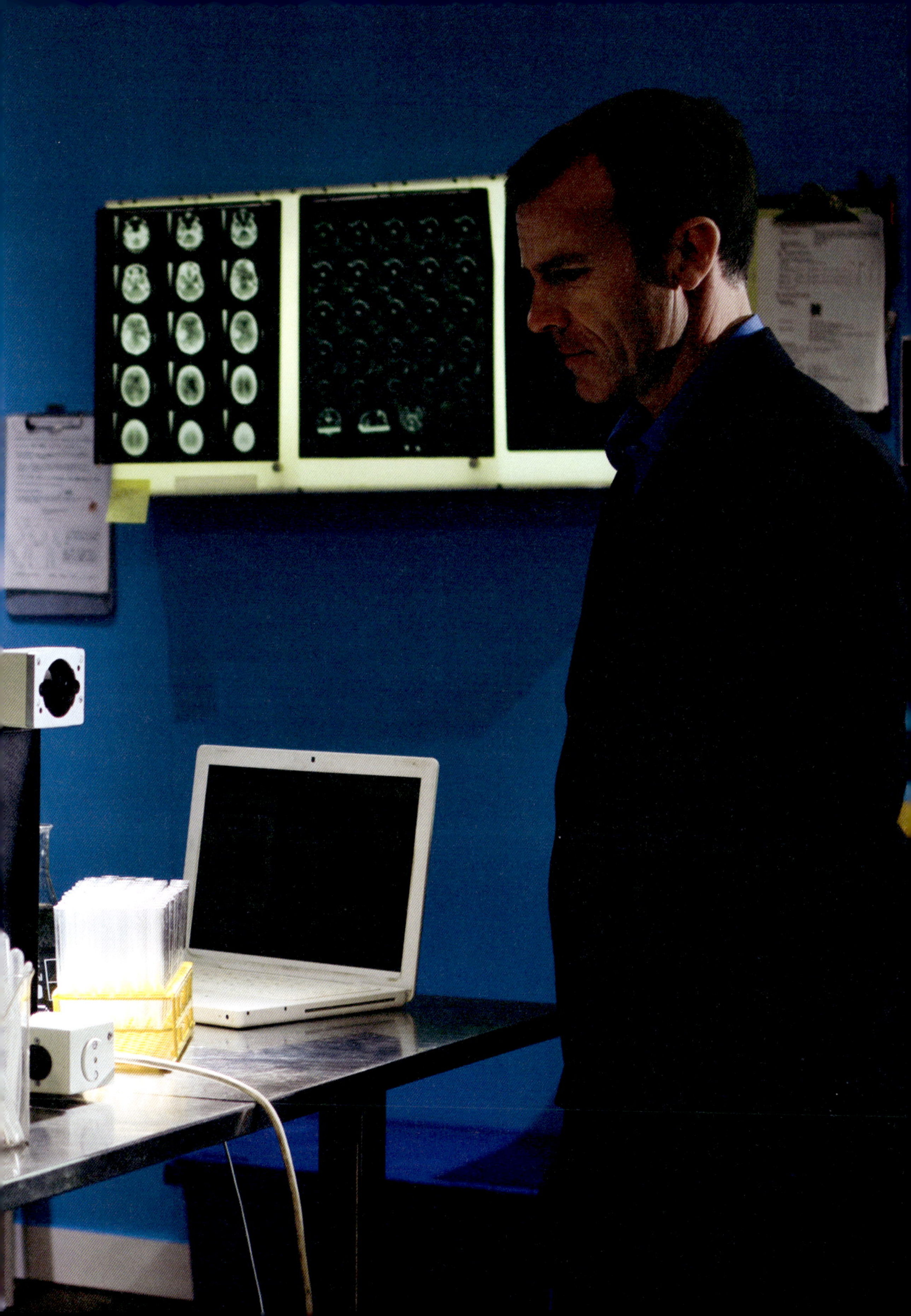

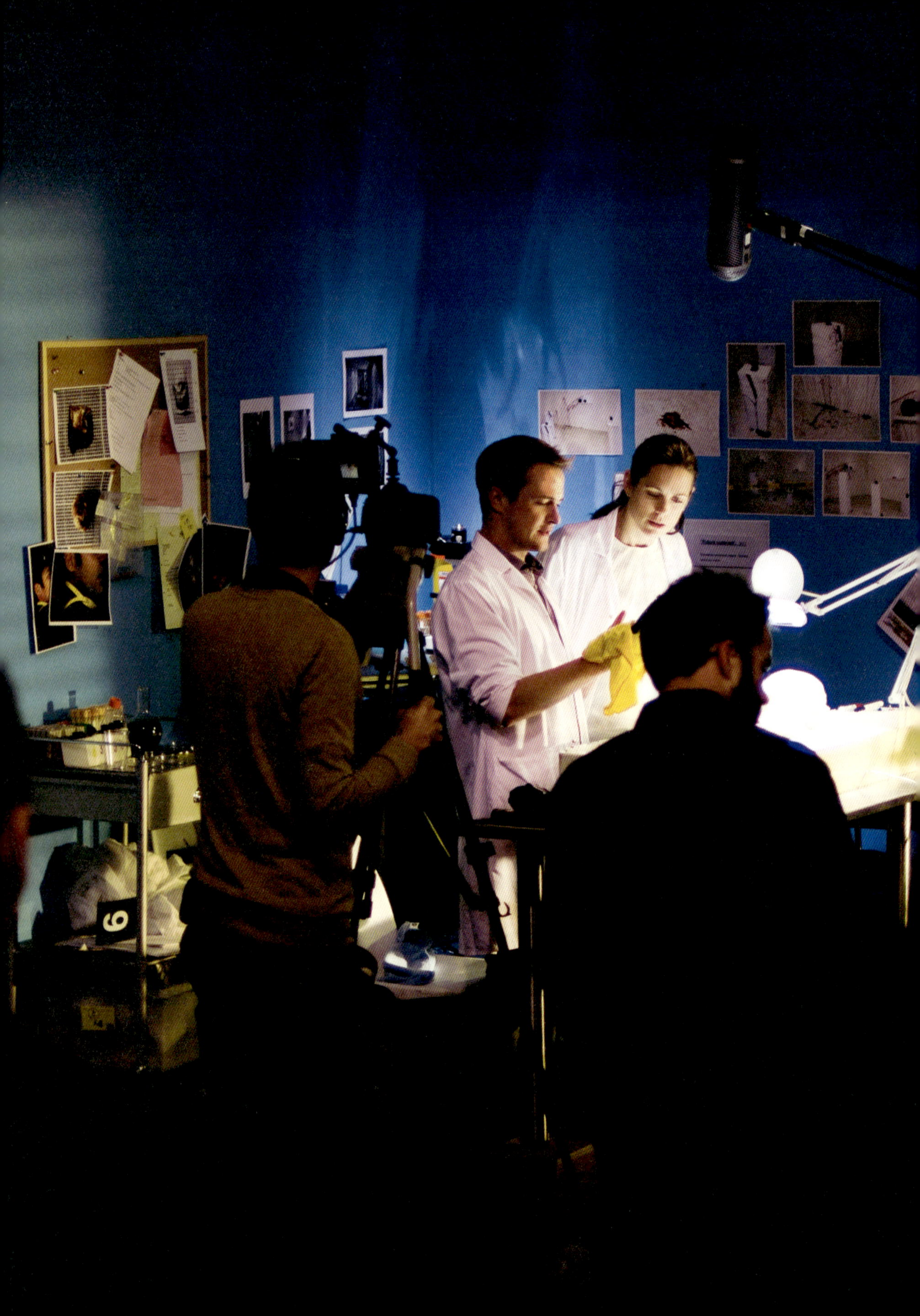

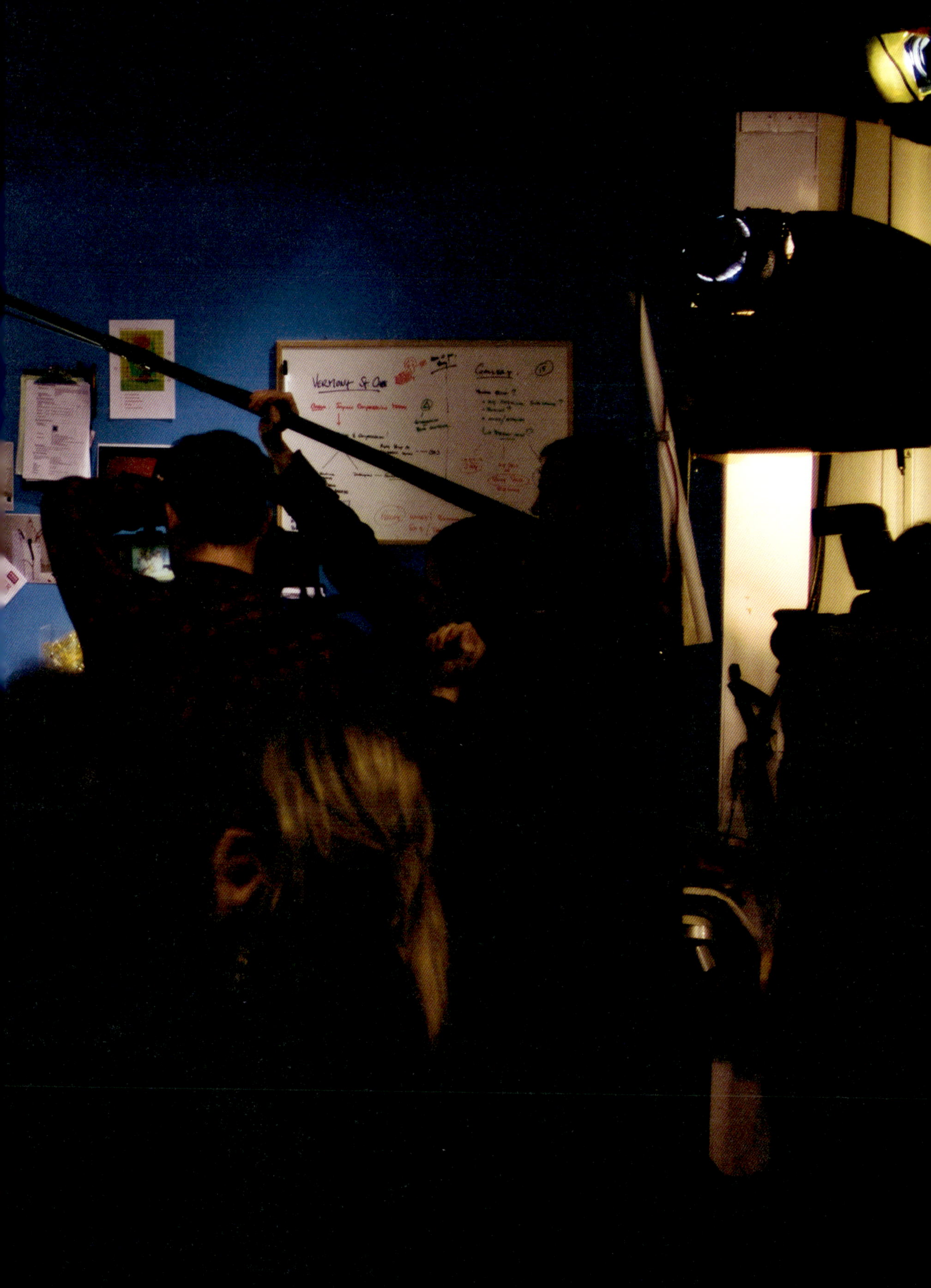

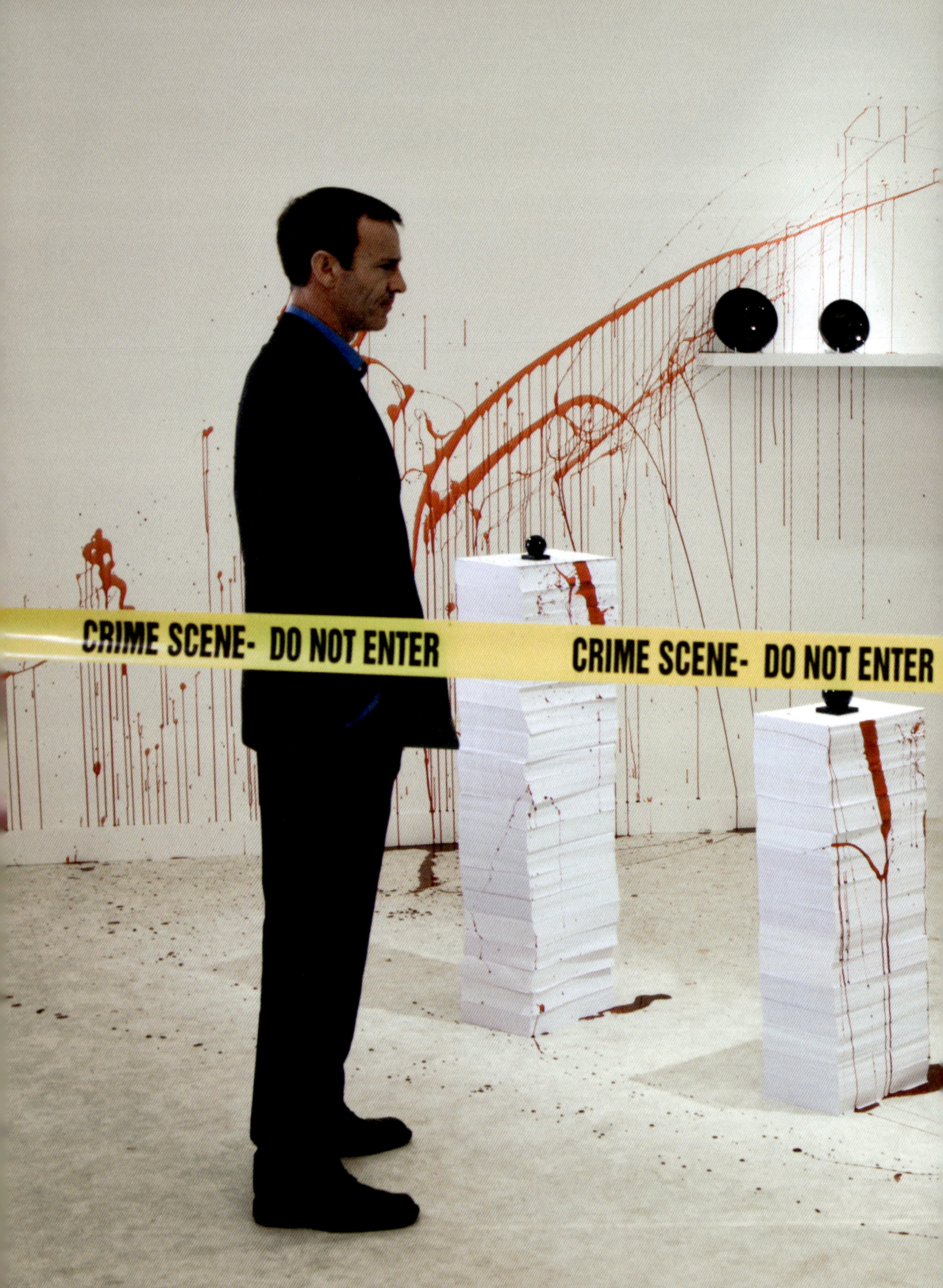

CRIME SCENE- DO NOT ENTER
CRIME SCENE- DO NOT ENTER

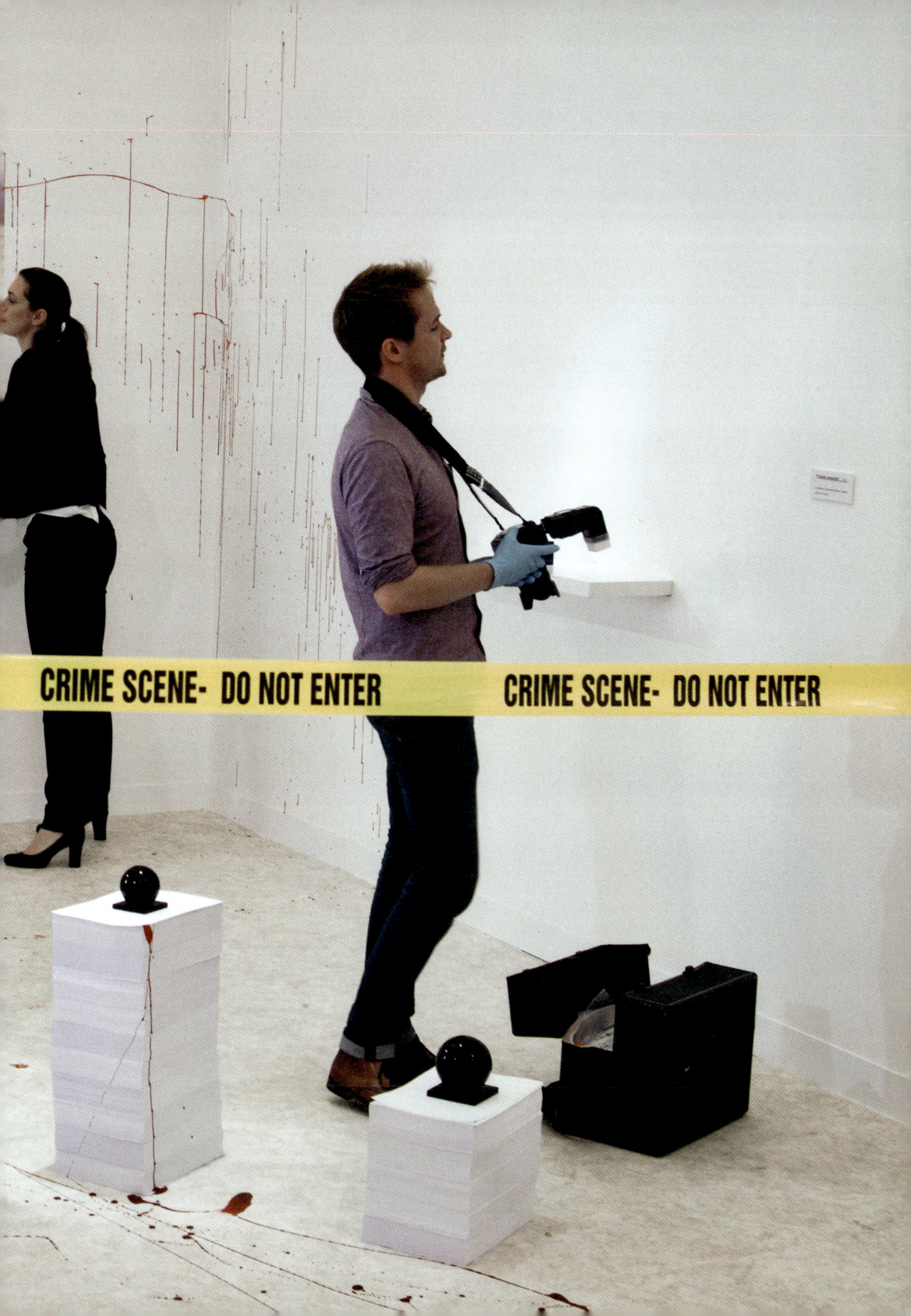

CRIME SCENE- DO NOT ENTER
CRIME SCENE- DO NOT ENTER

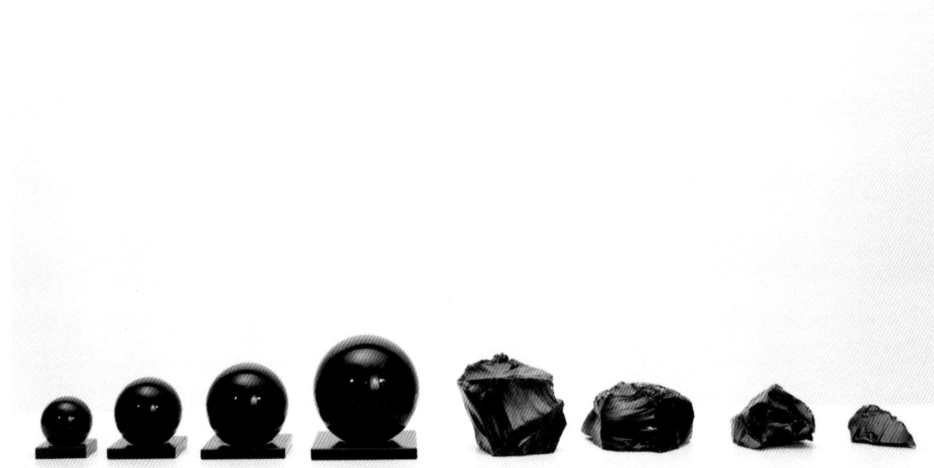

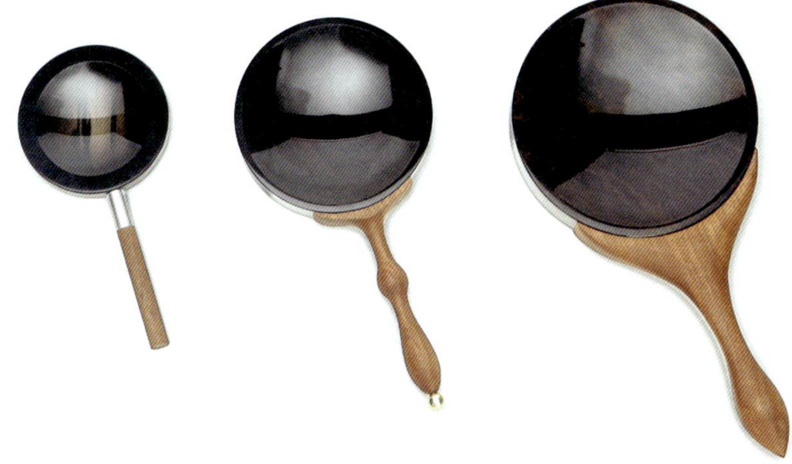

Gordian Knot, 2013

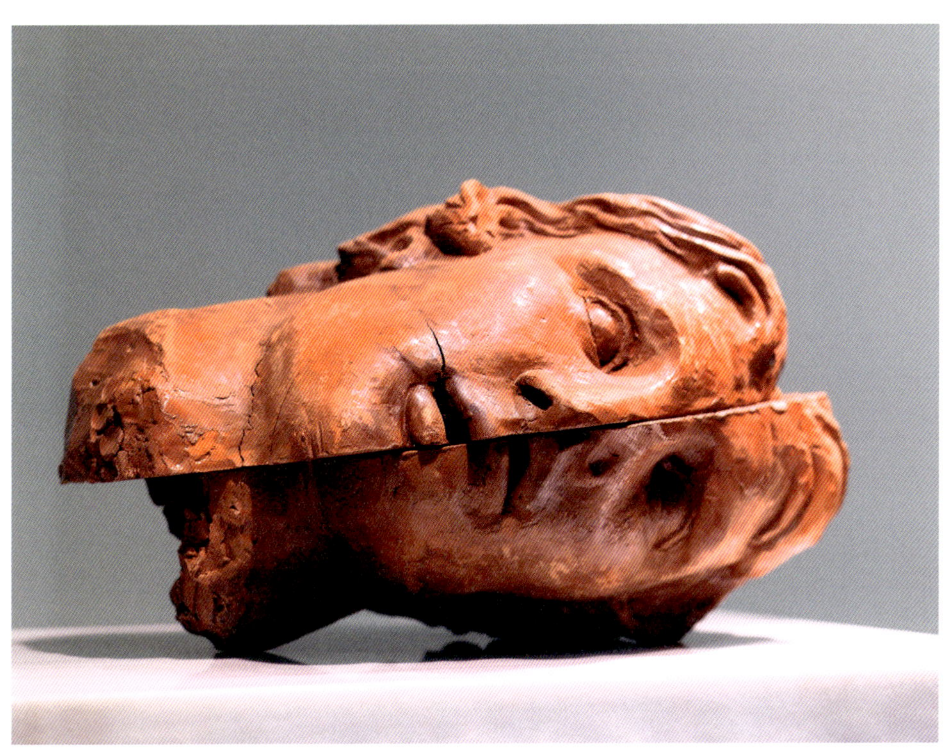

71

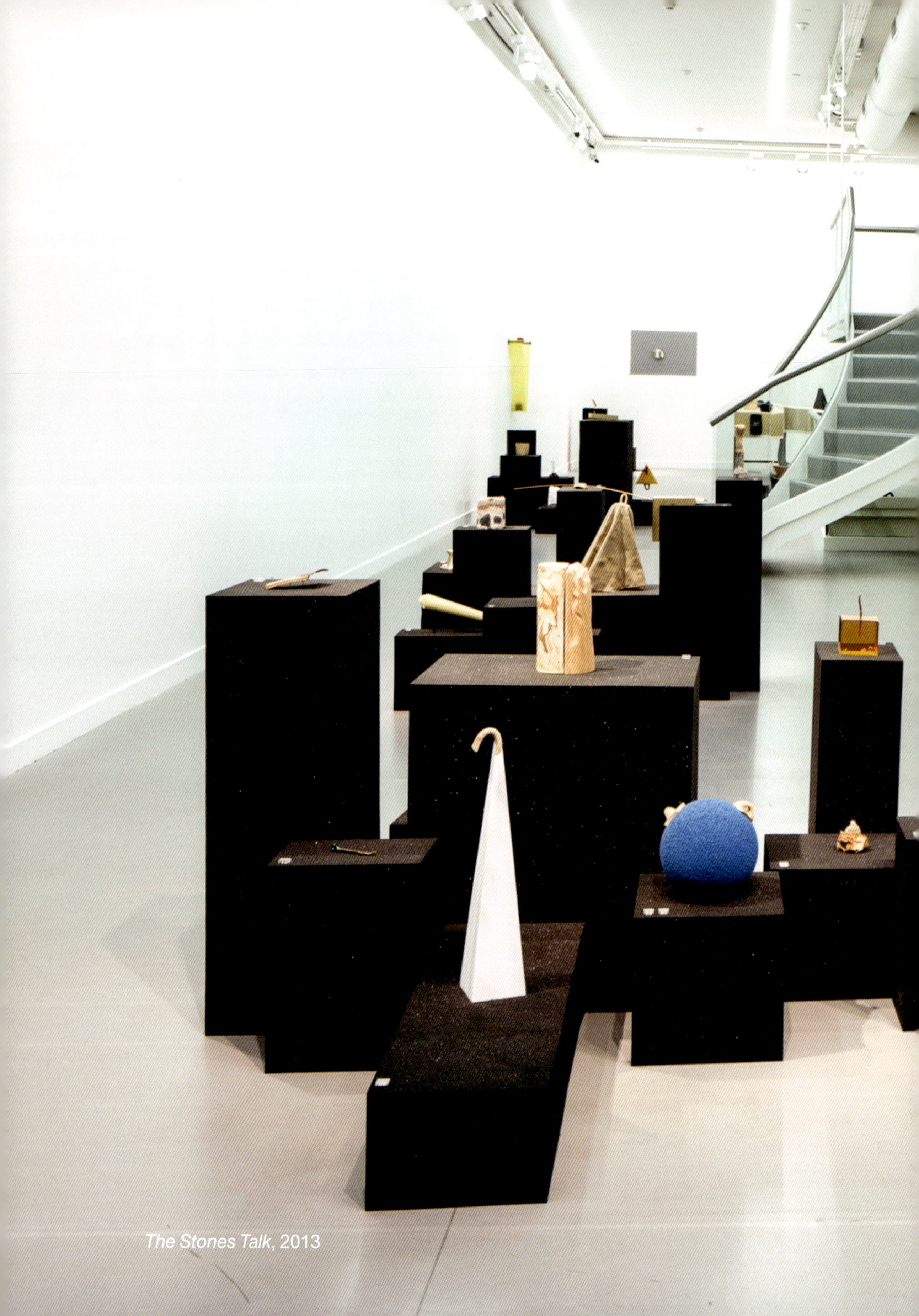

The Stones Talk, 2013

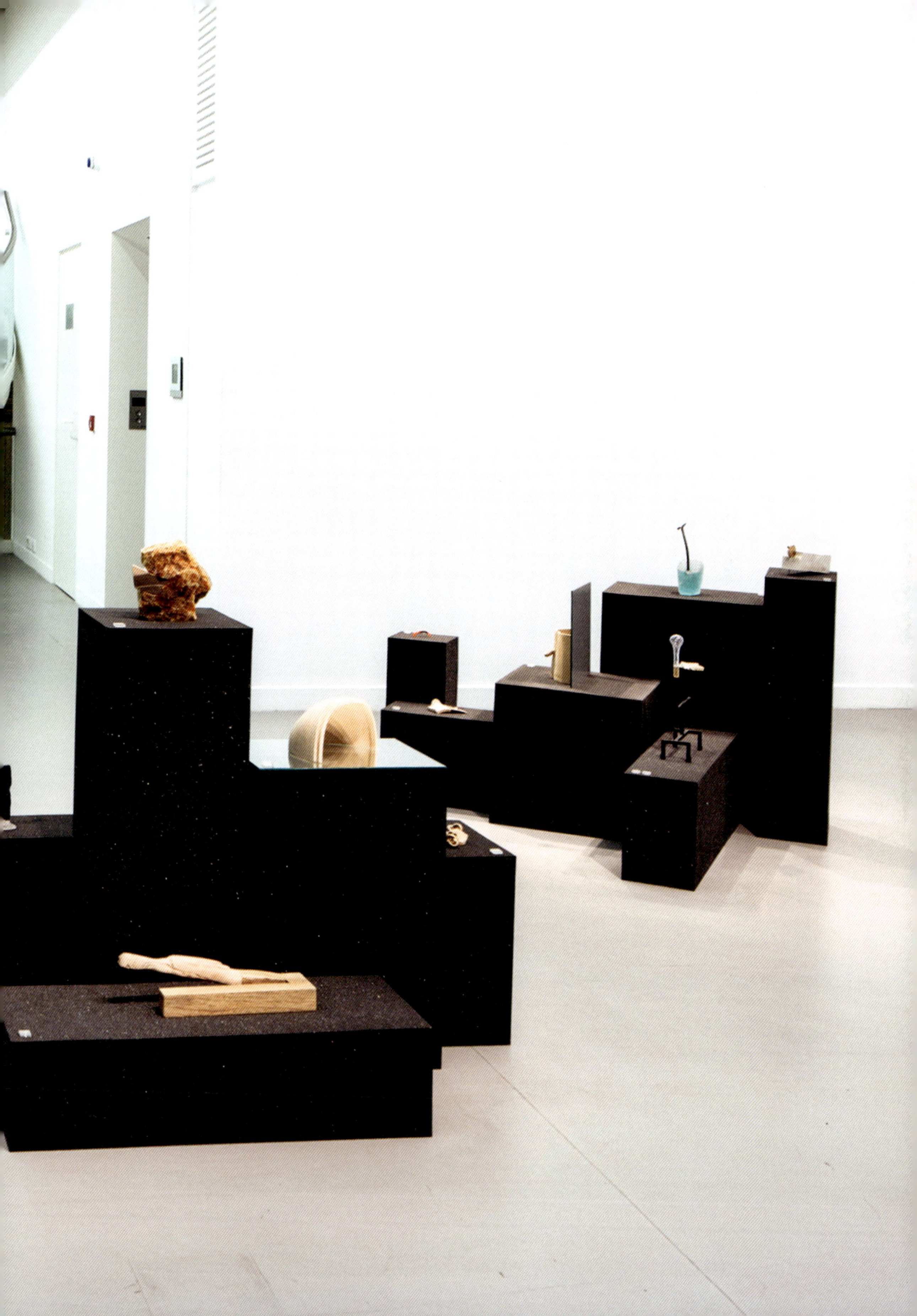

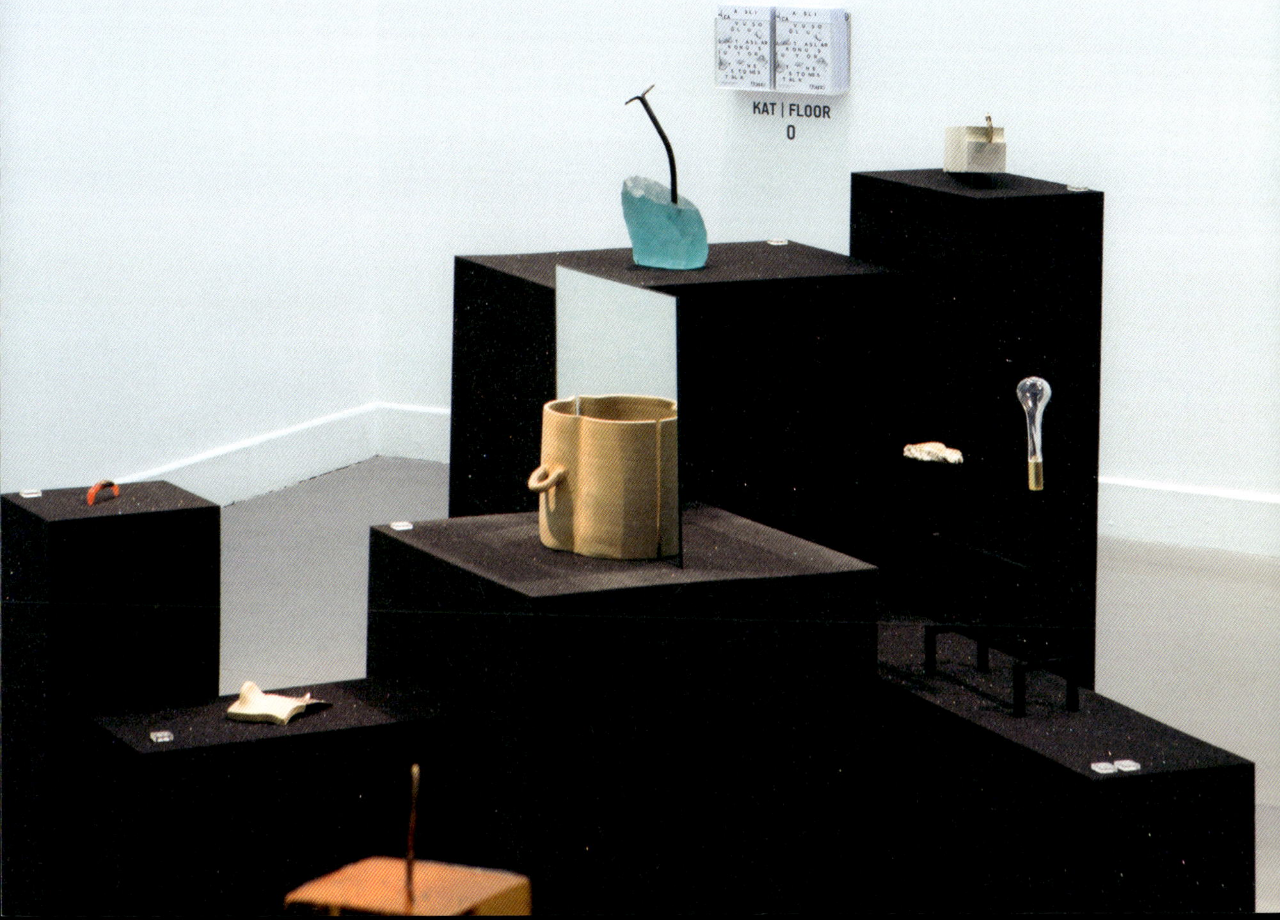

ASLI
ÇAVUŞOĞLU
TAŞLAR KONUŞUYOR
THE STONES TALK
KÜRATÖR | CURATOR
ÖZGE ERSOY
KAT | FLOOR
0

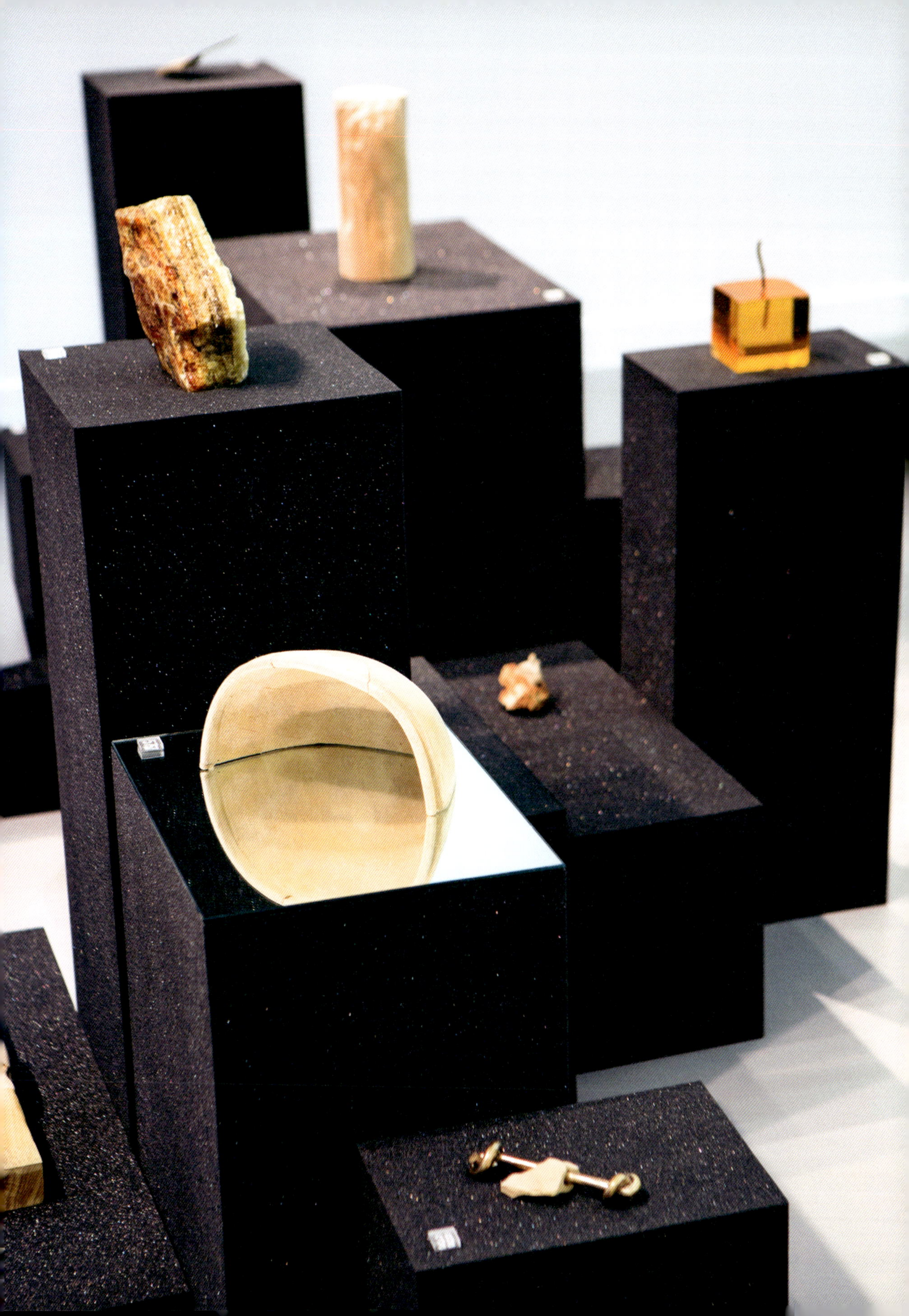

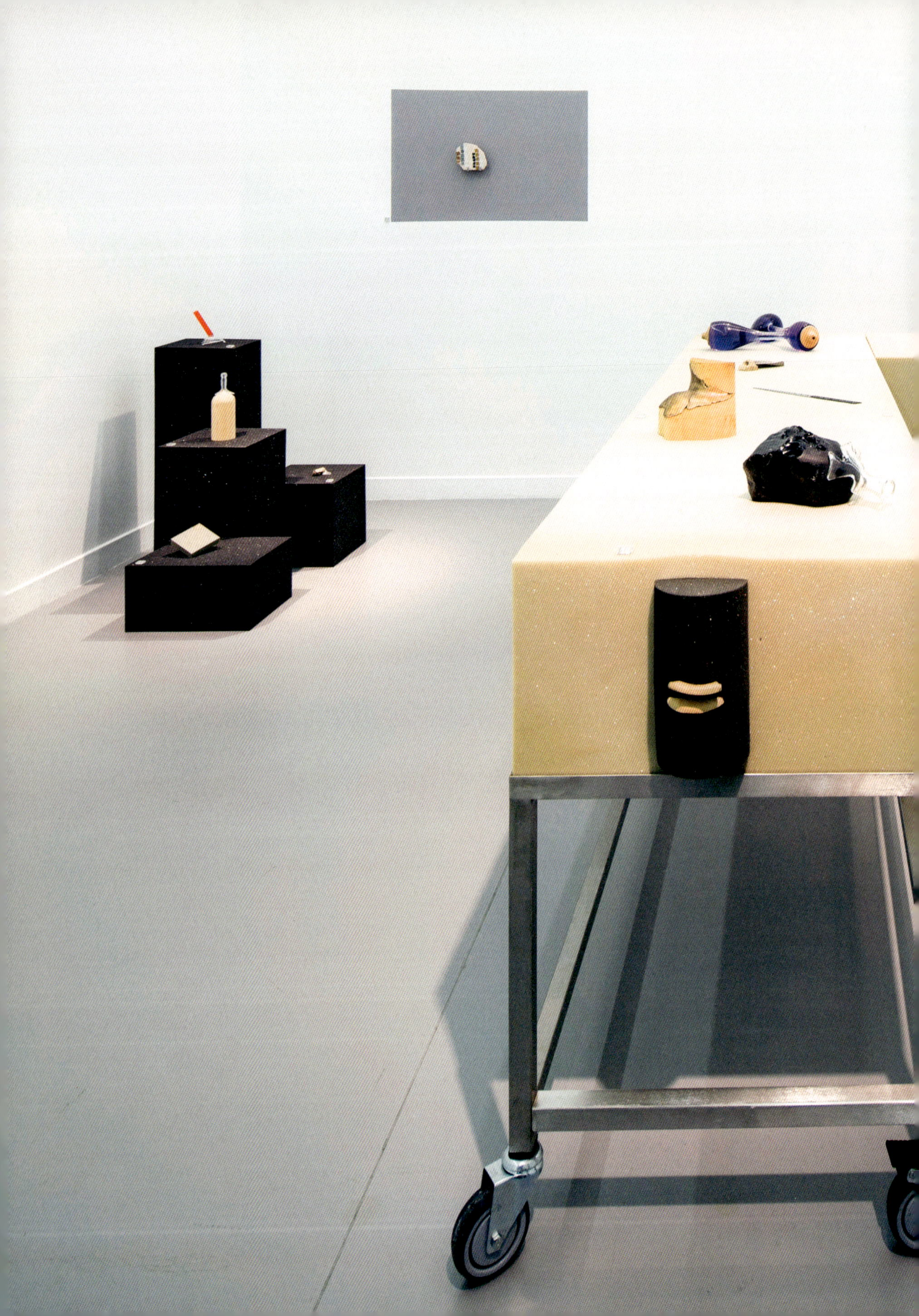

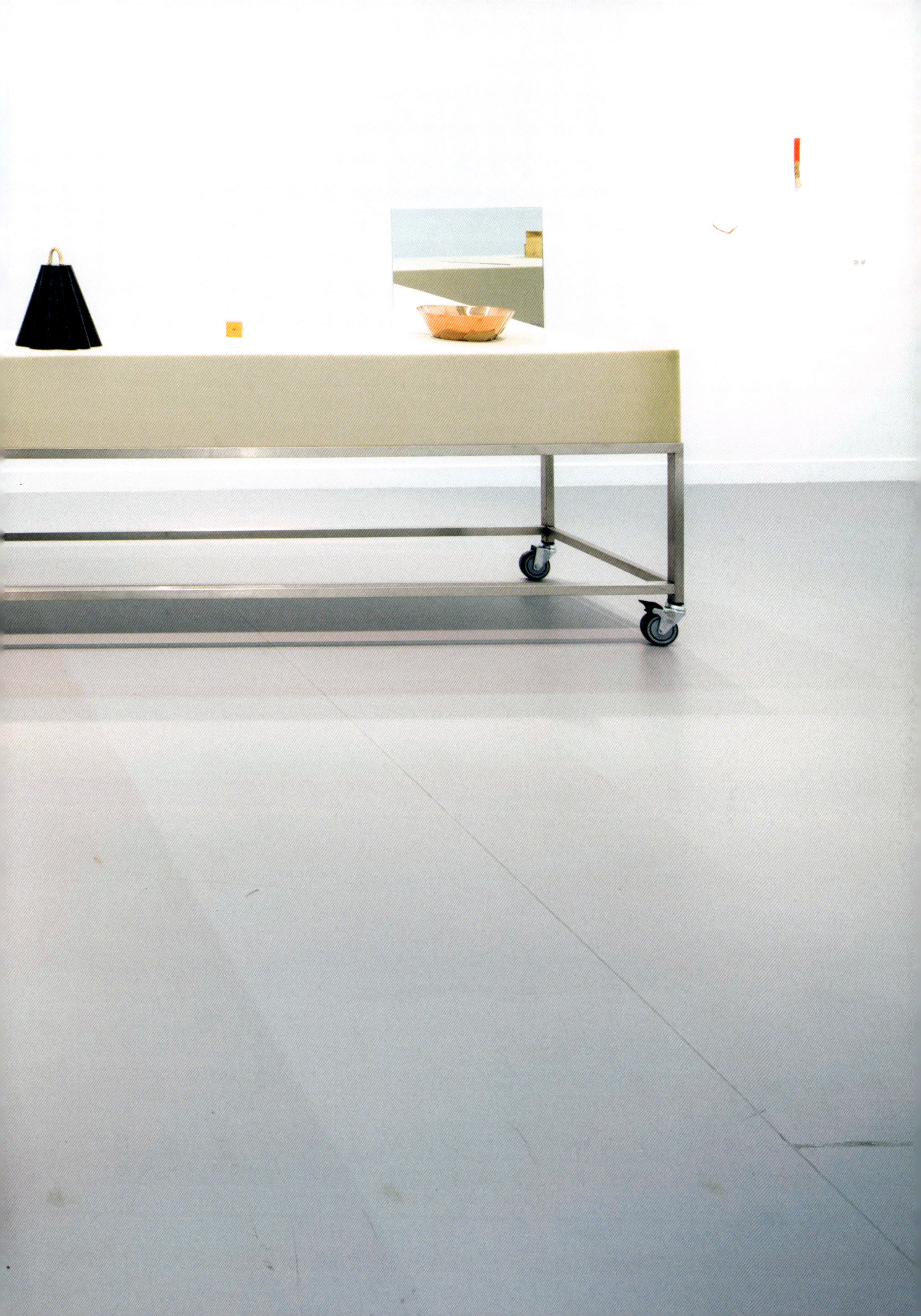

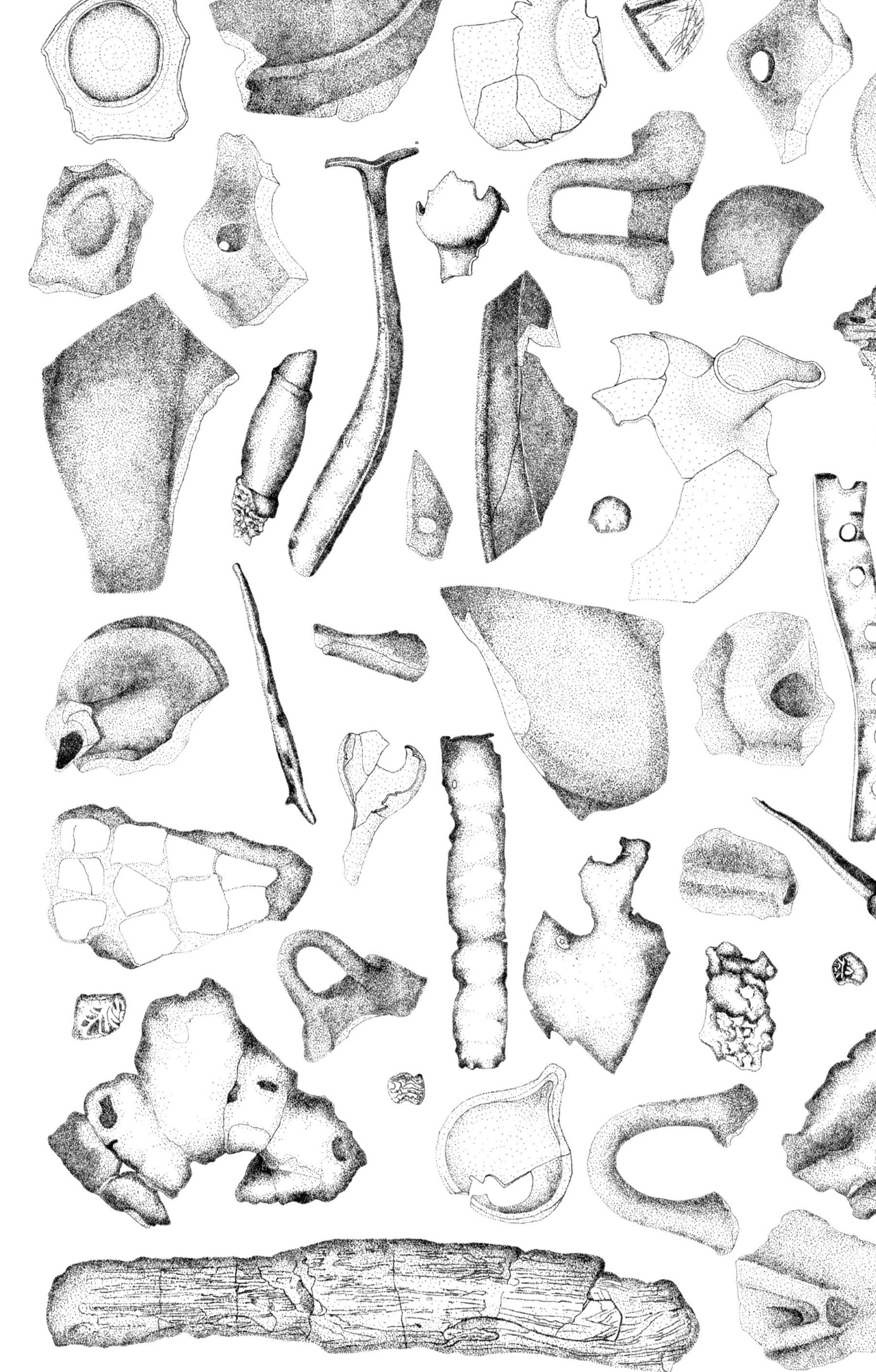

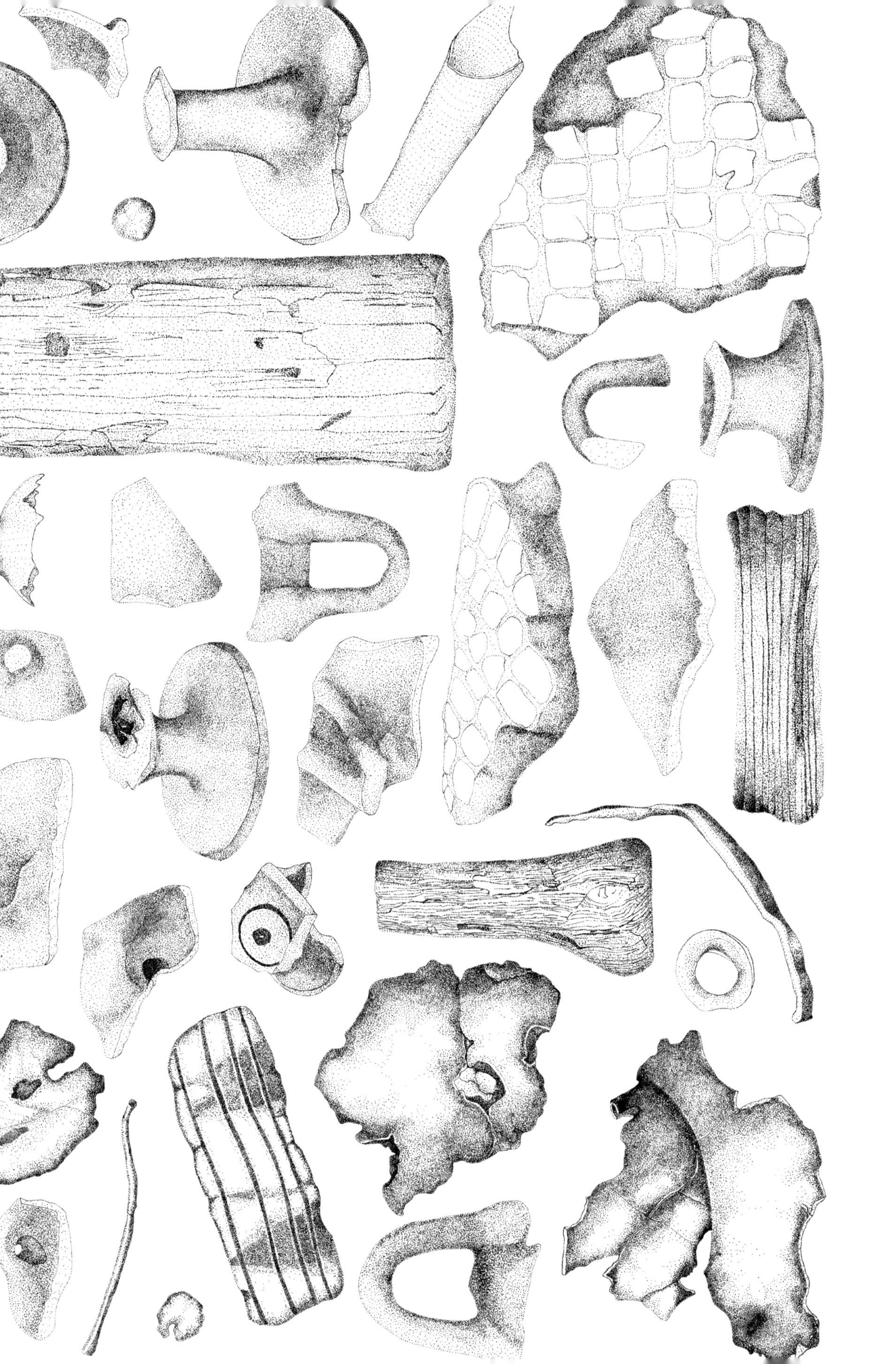

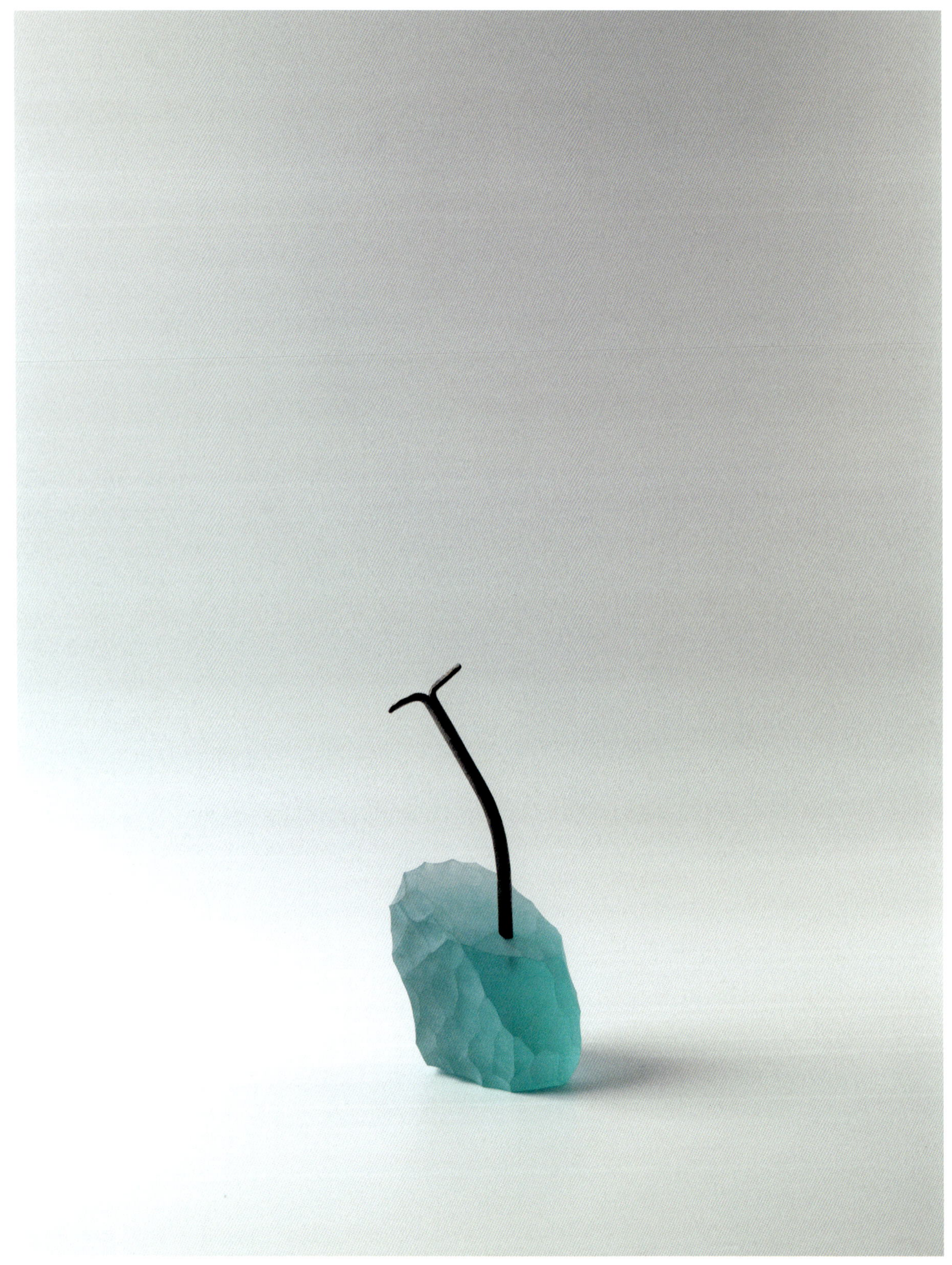

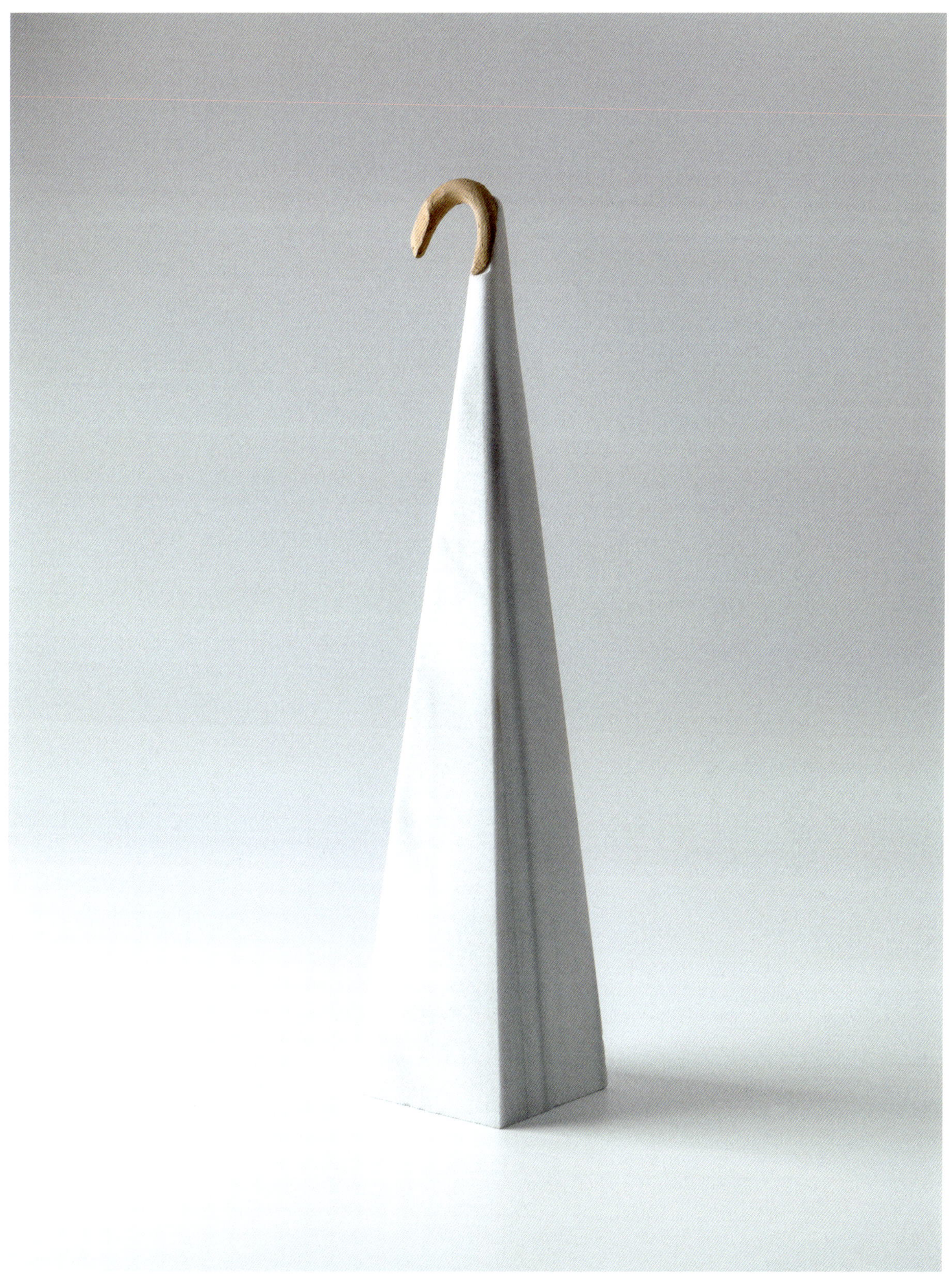

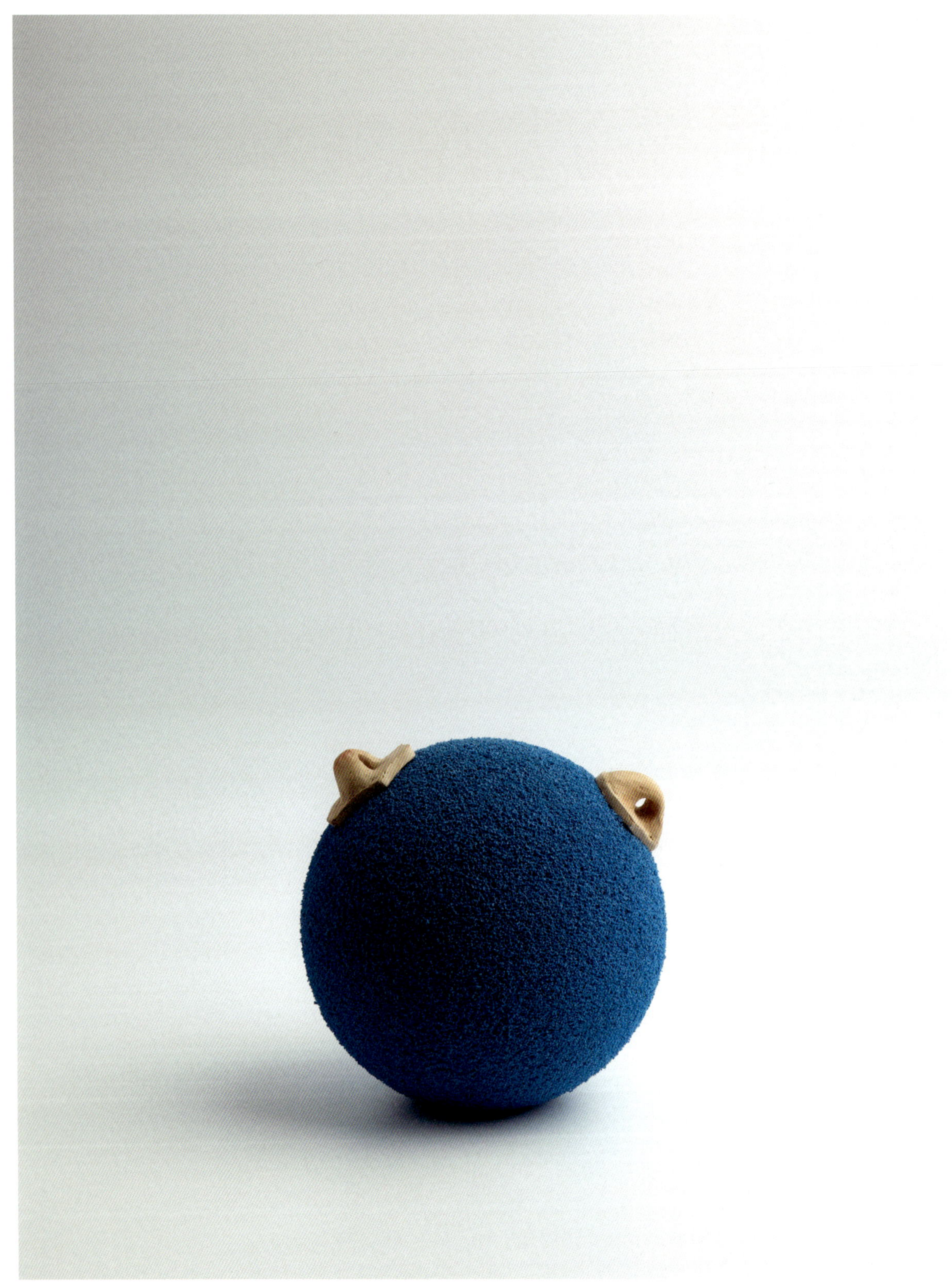

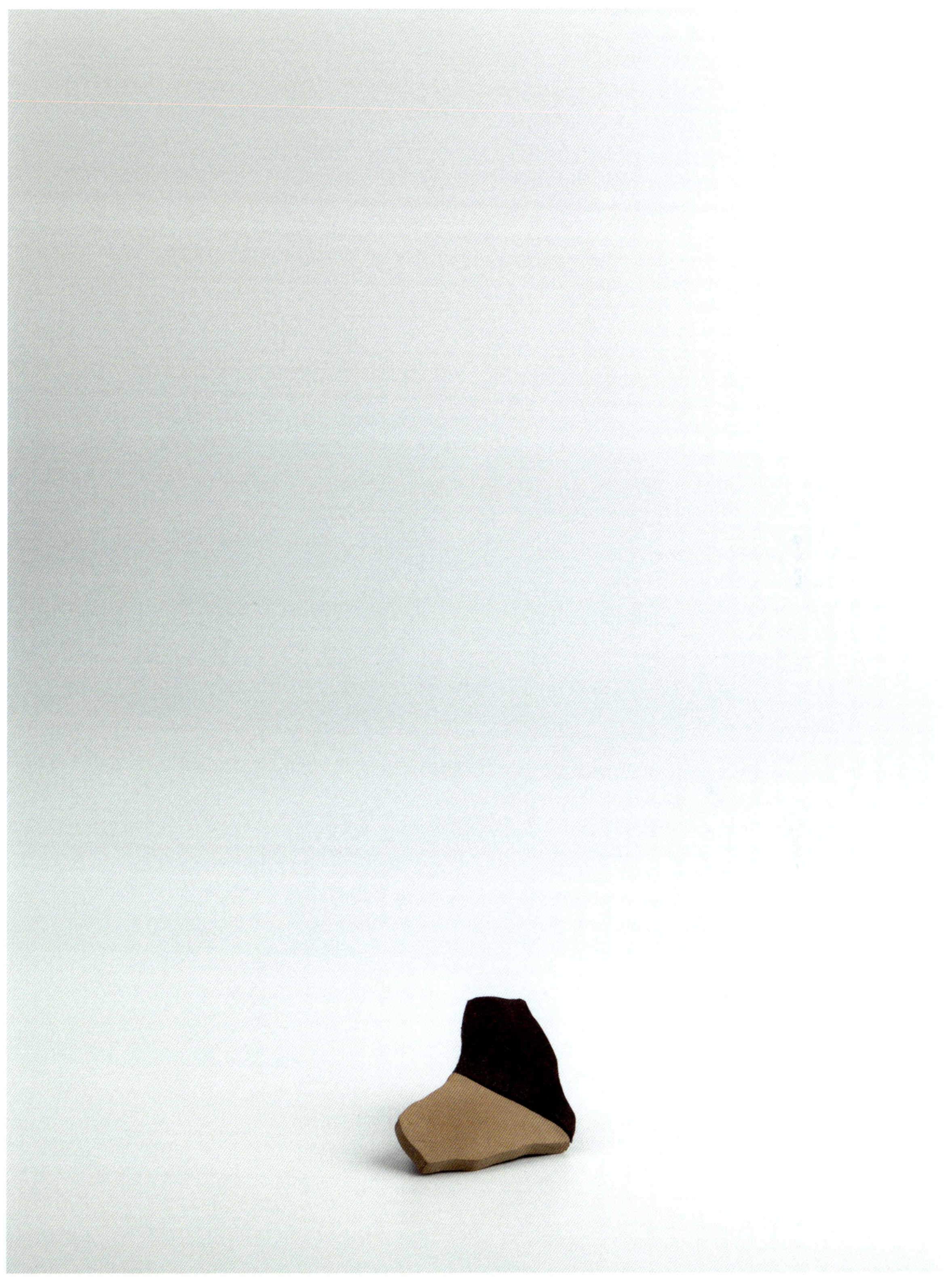

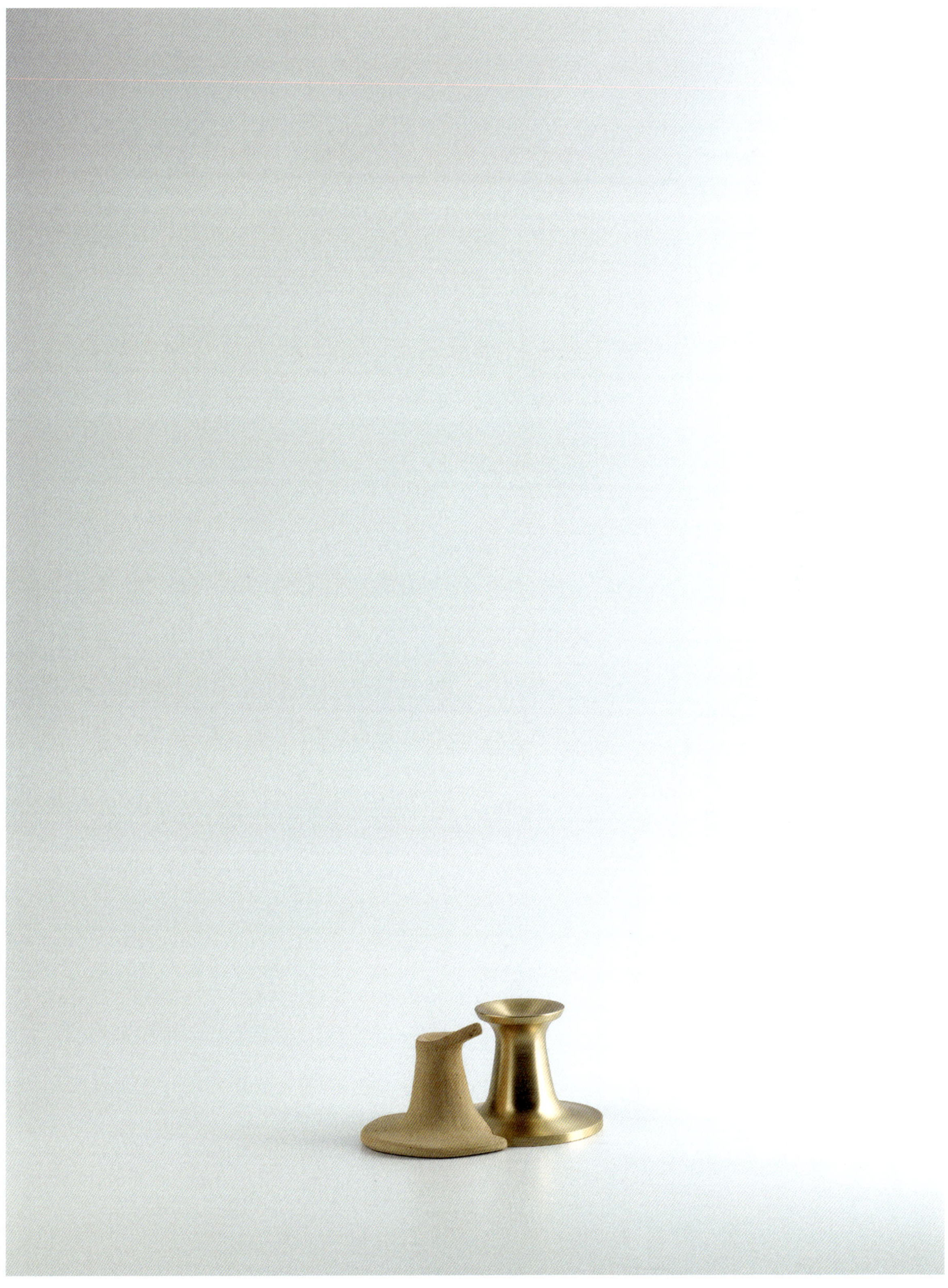

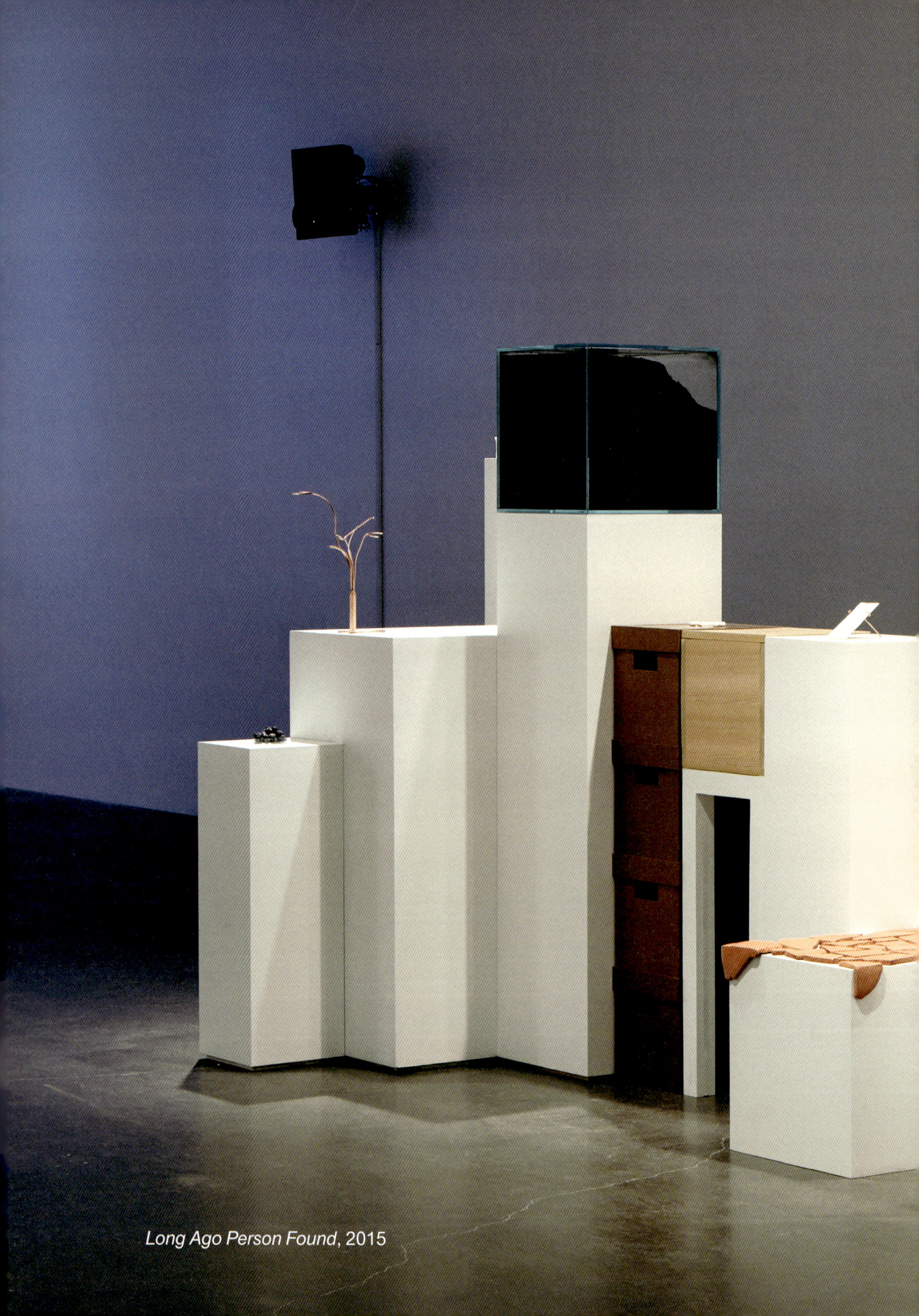

Long Ago Person Found, 2015

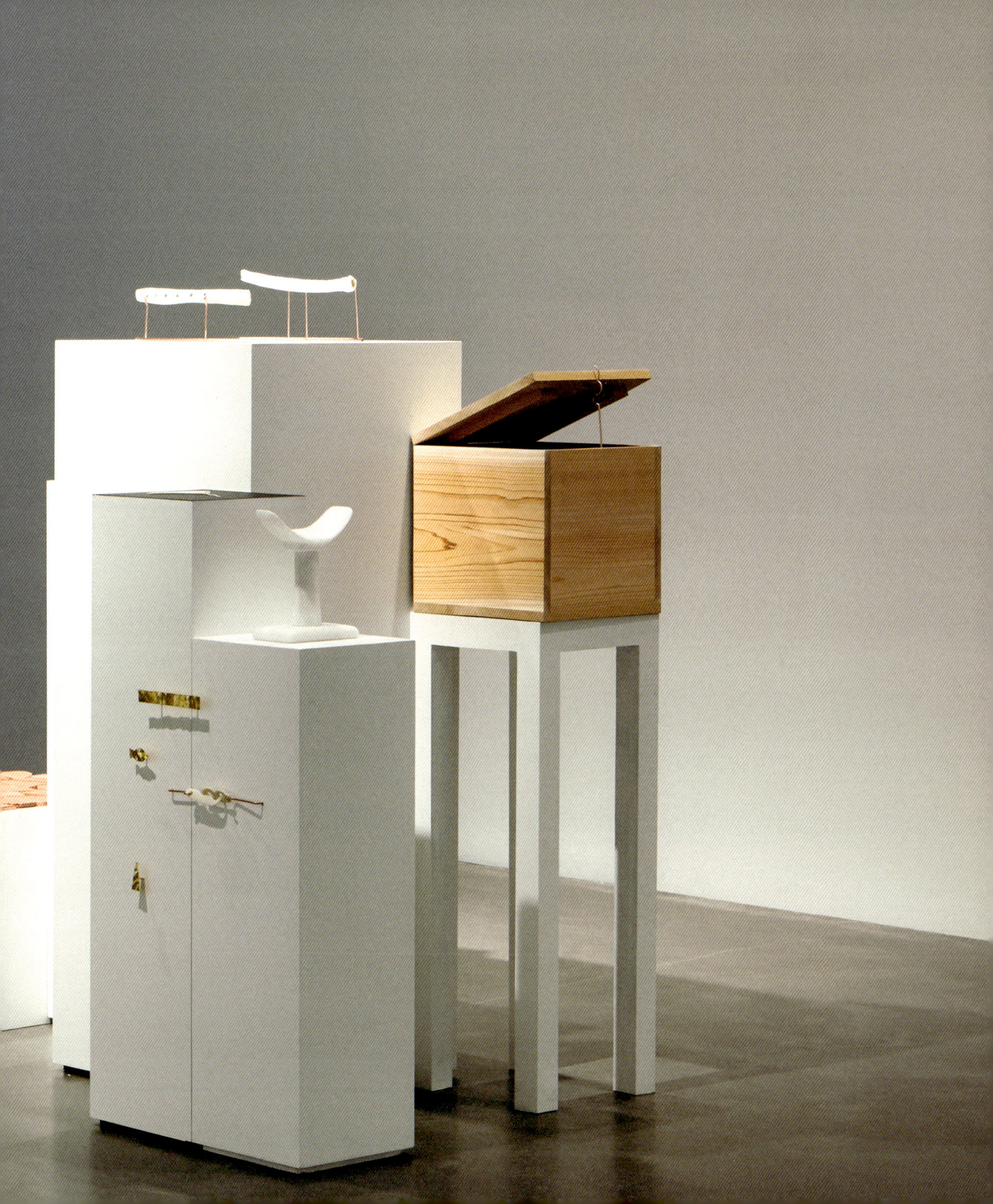

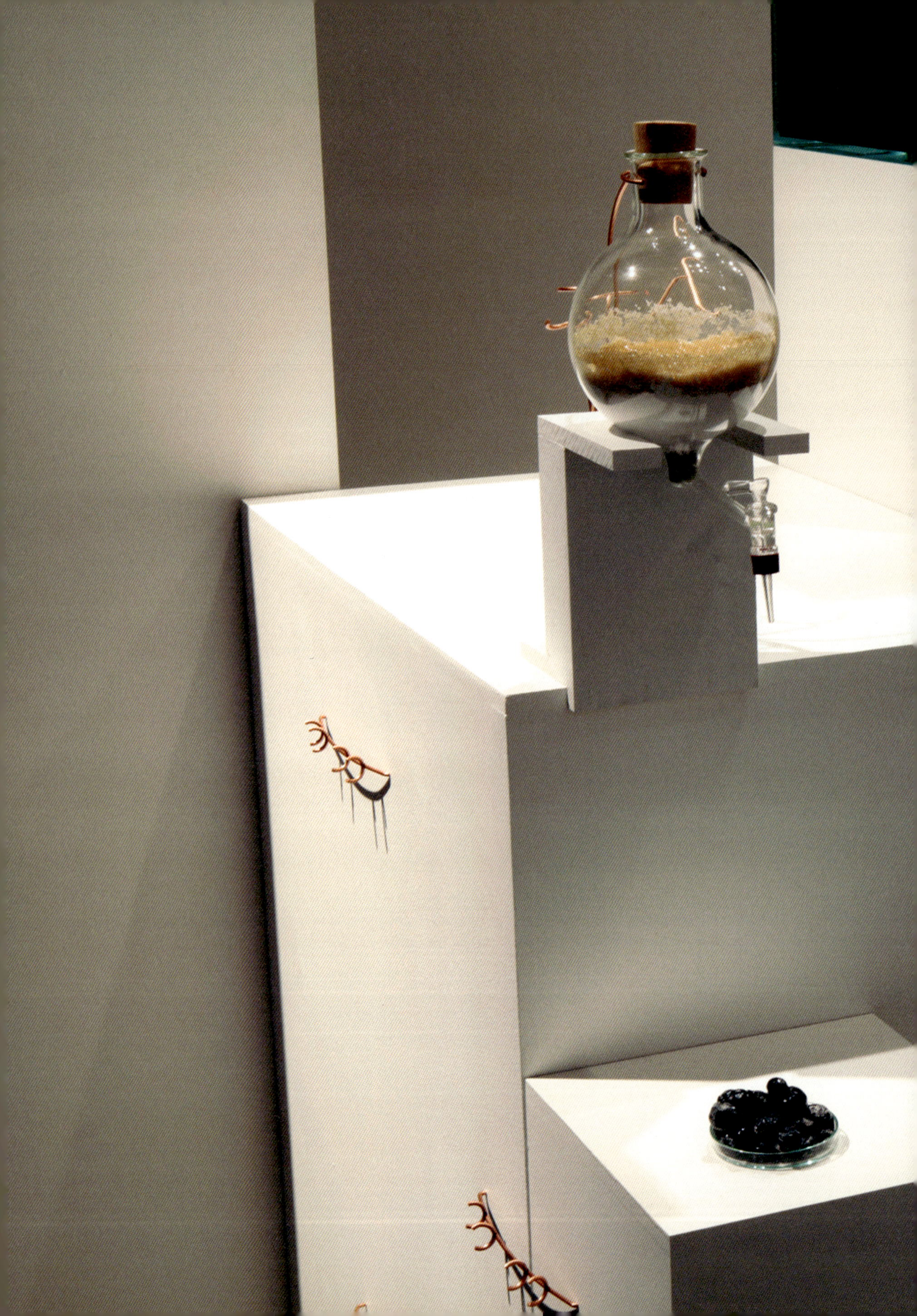

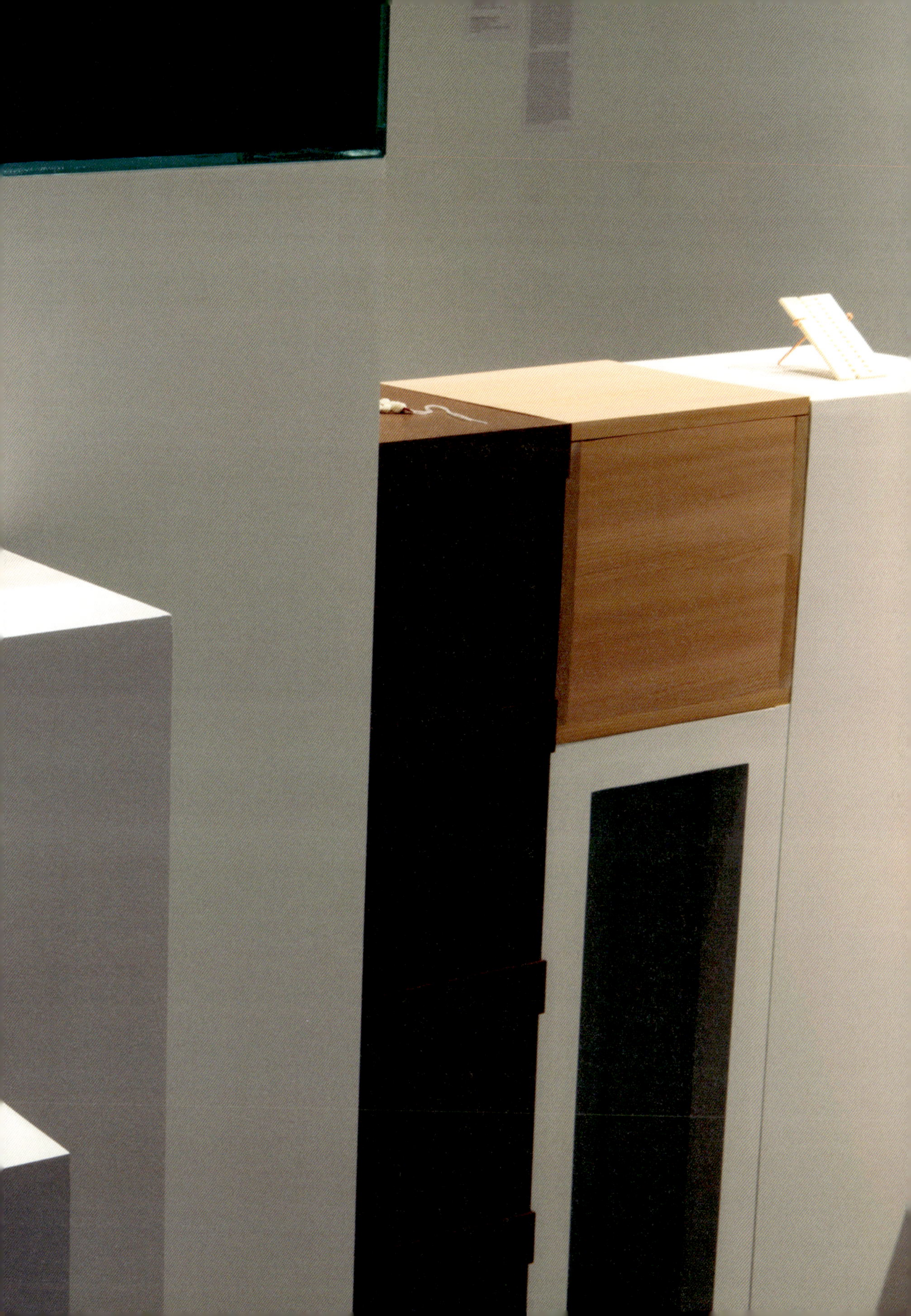

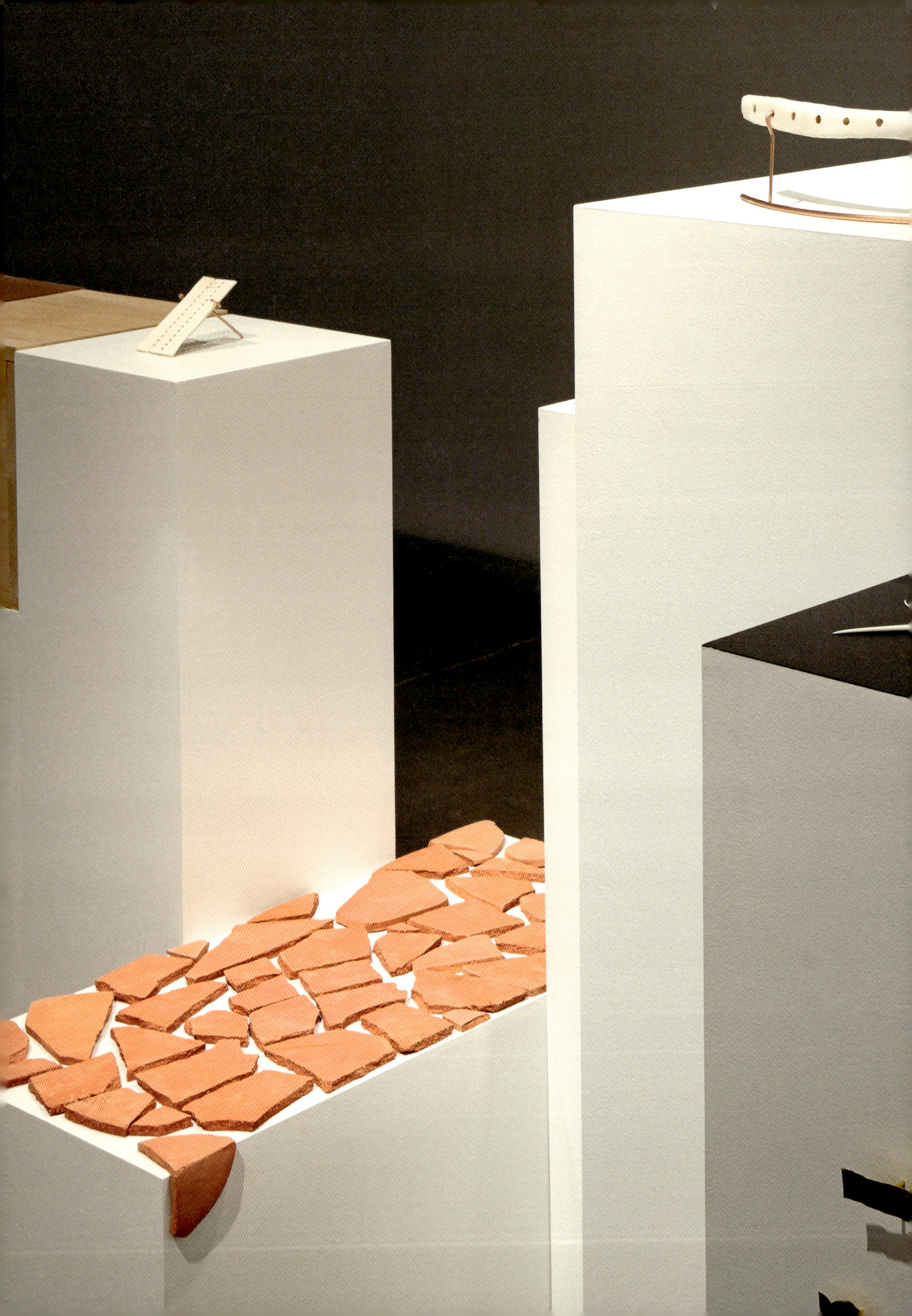

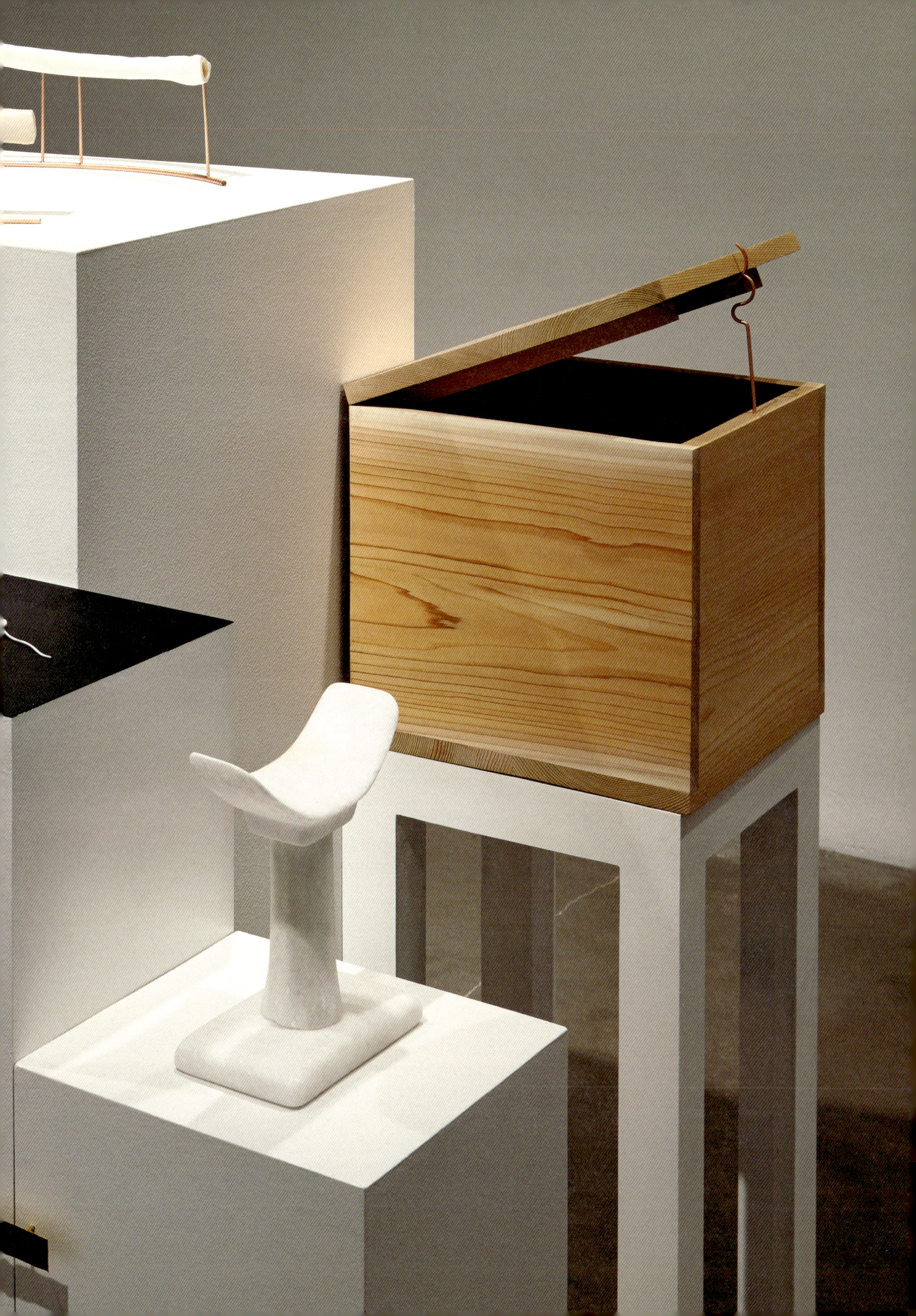

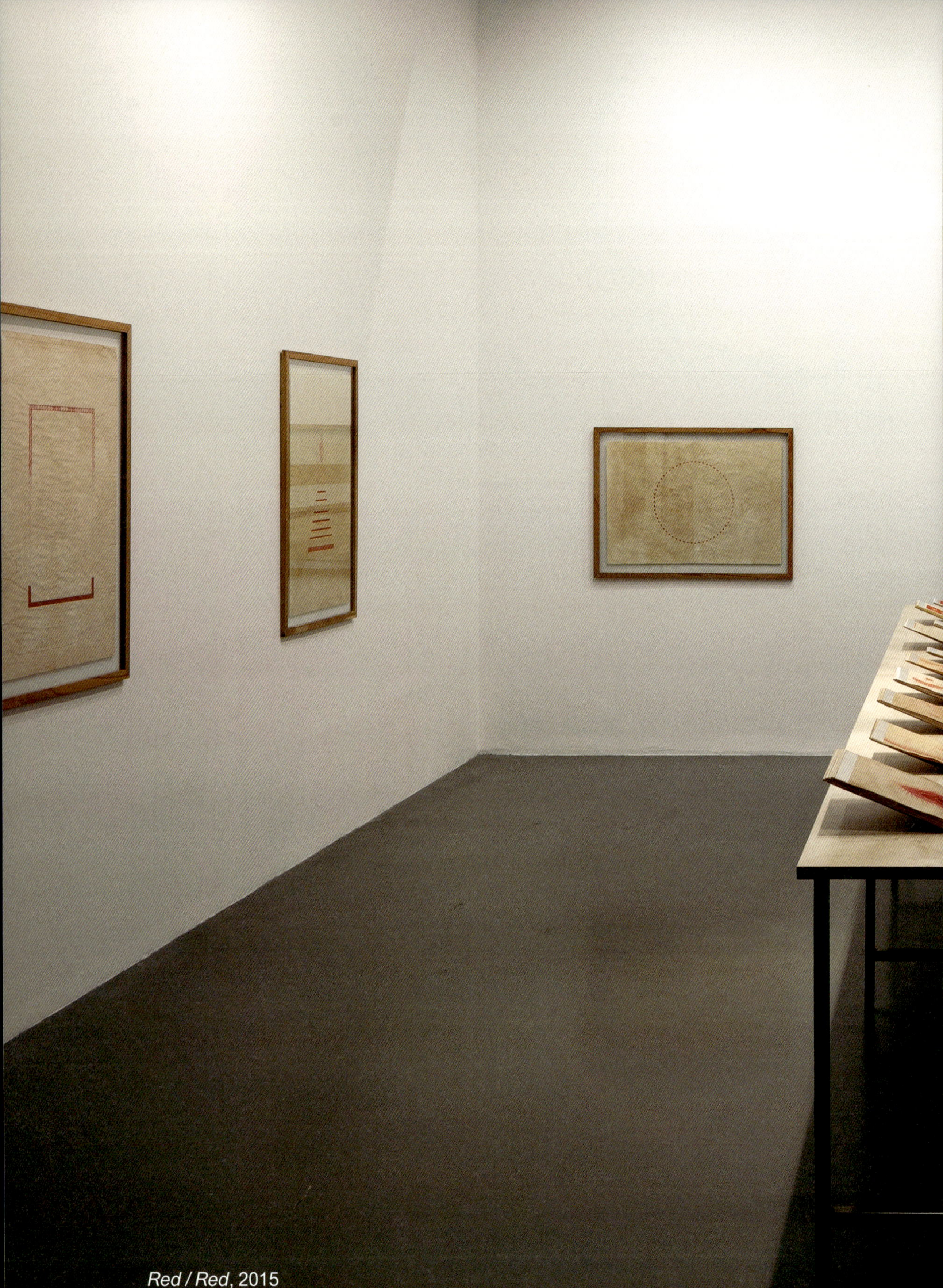

Red / Red, 2015

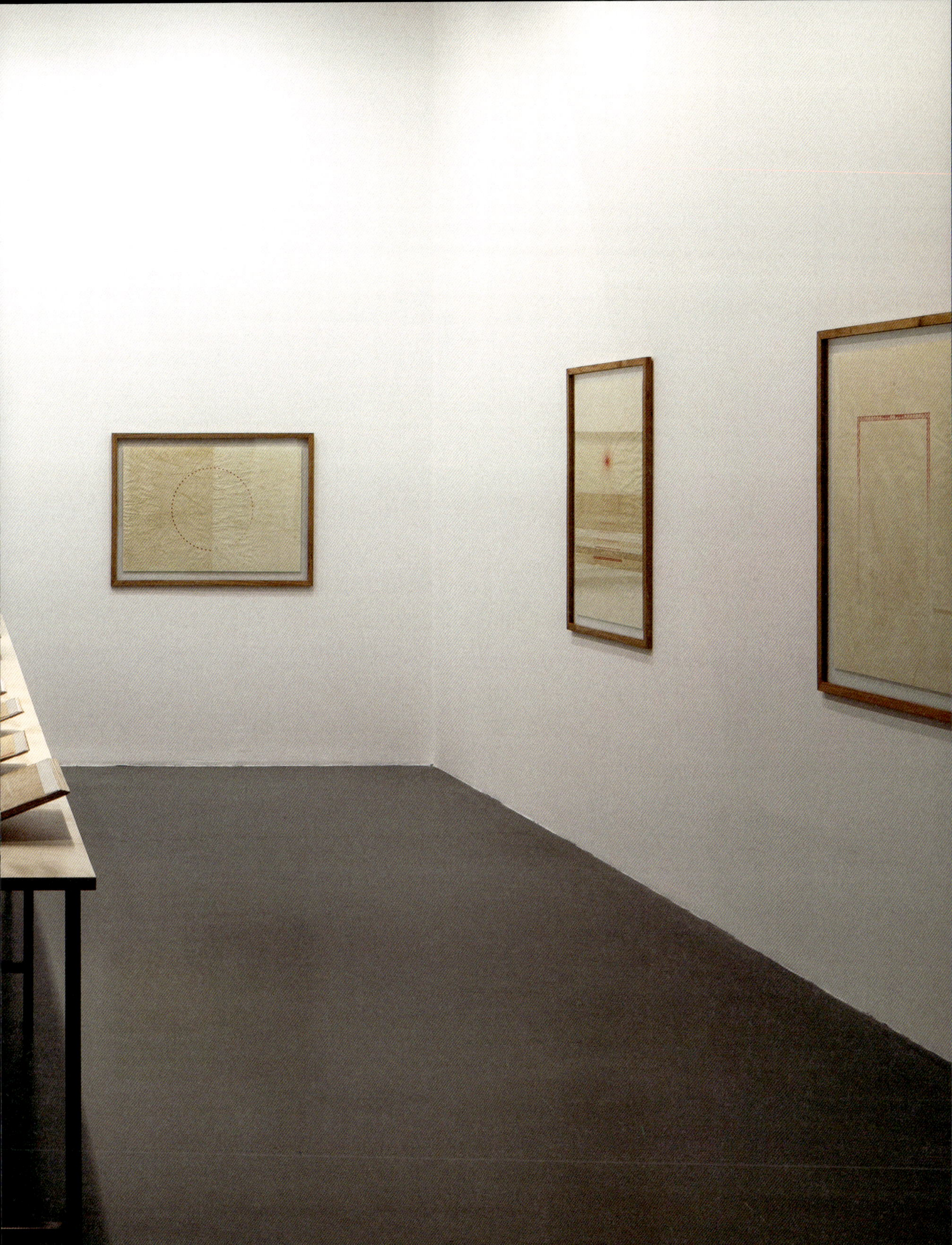

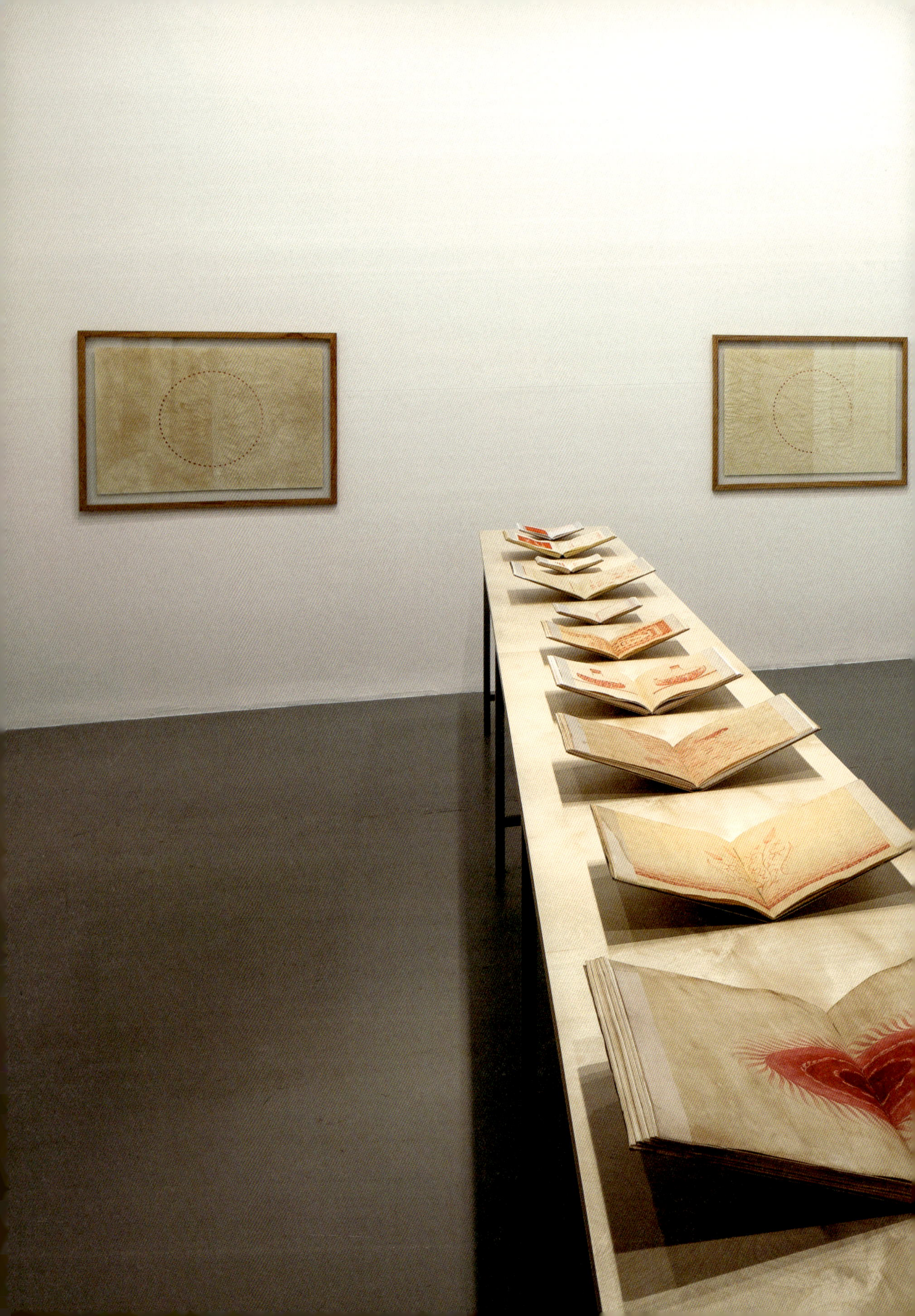

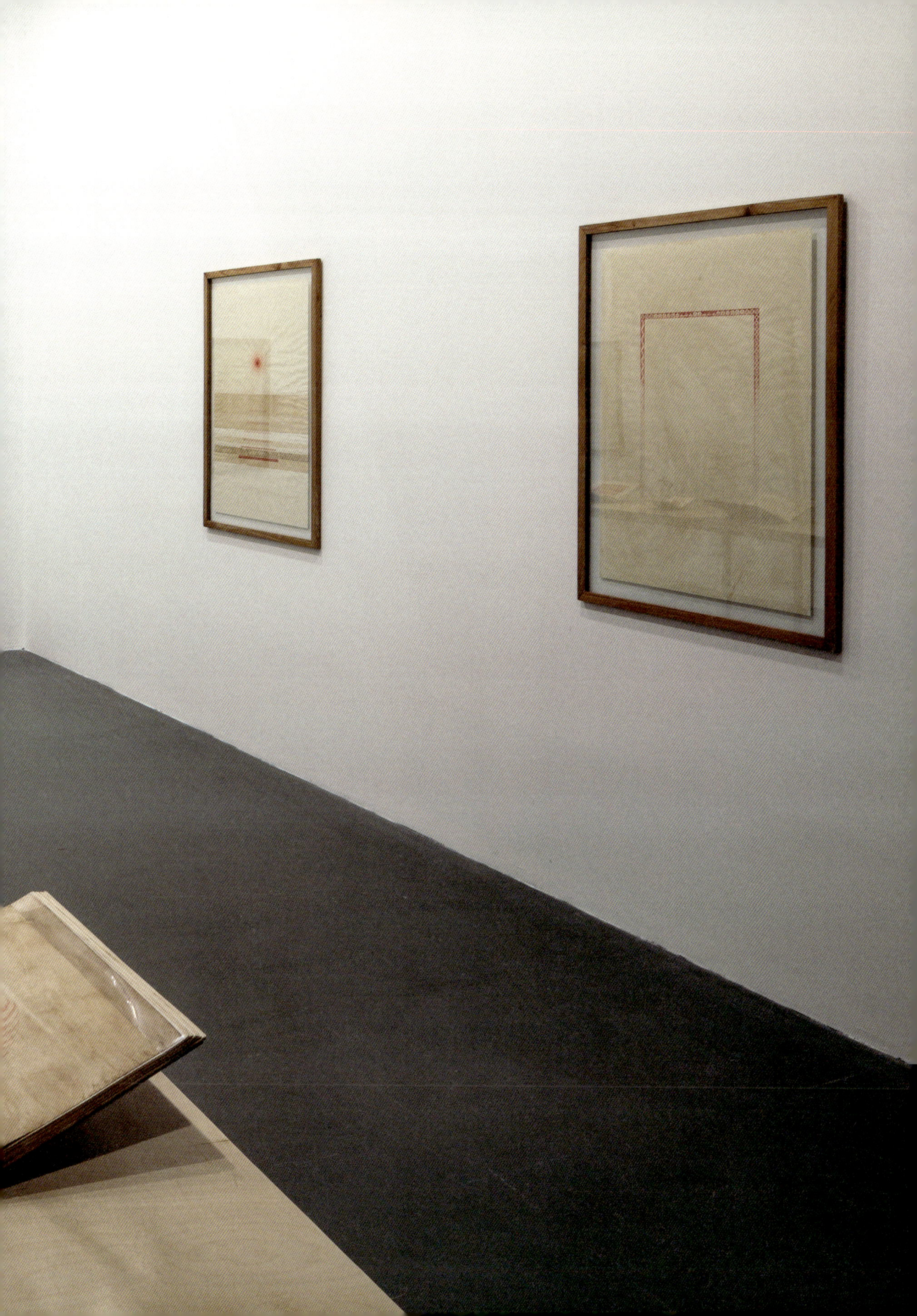

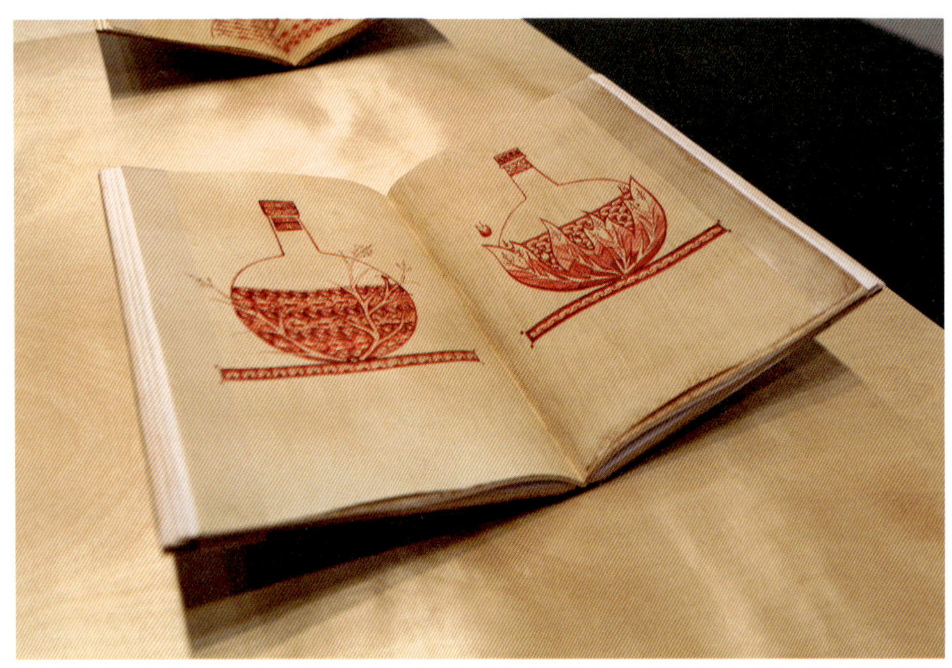

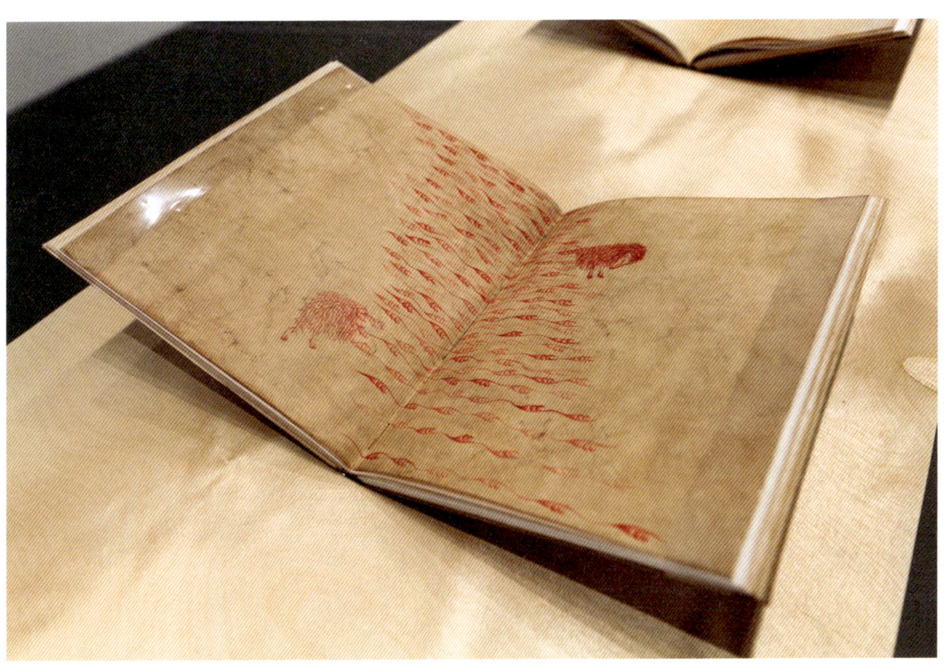

The Cut, 2015

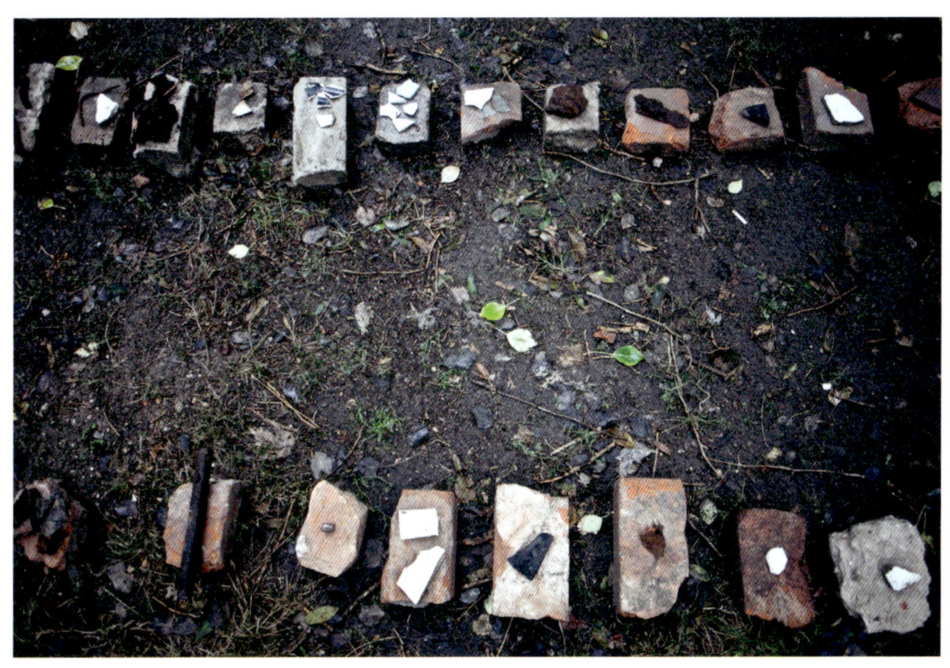

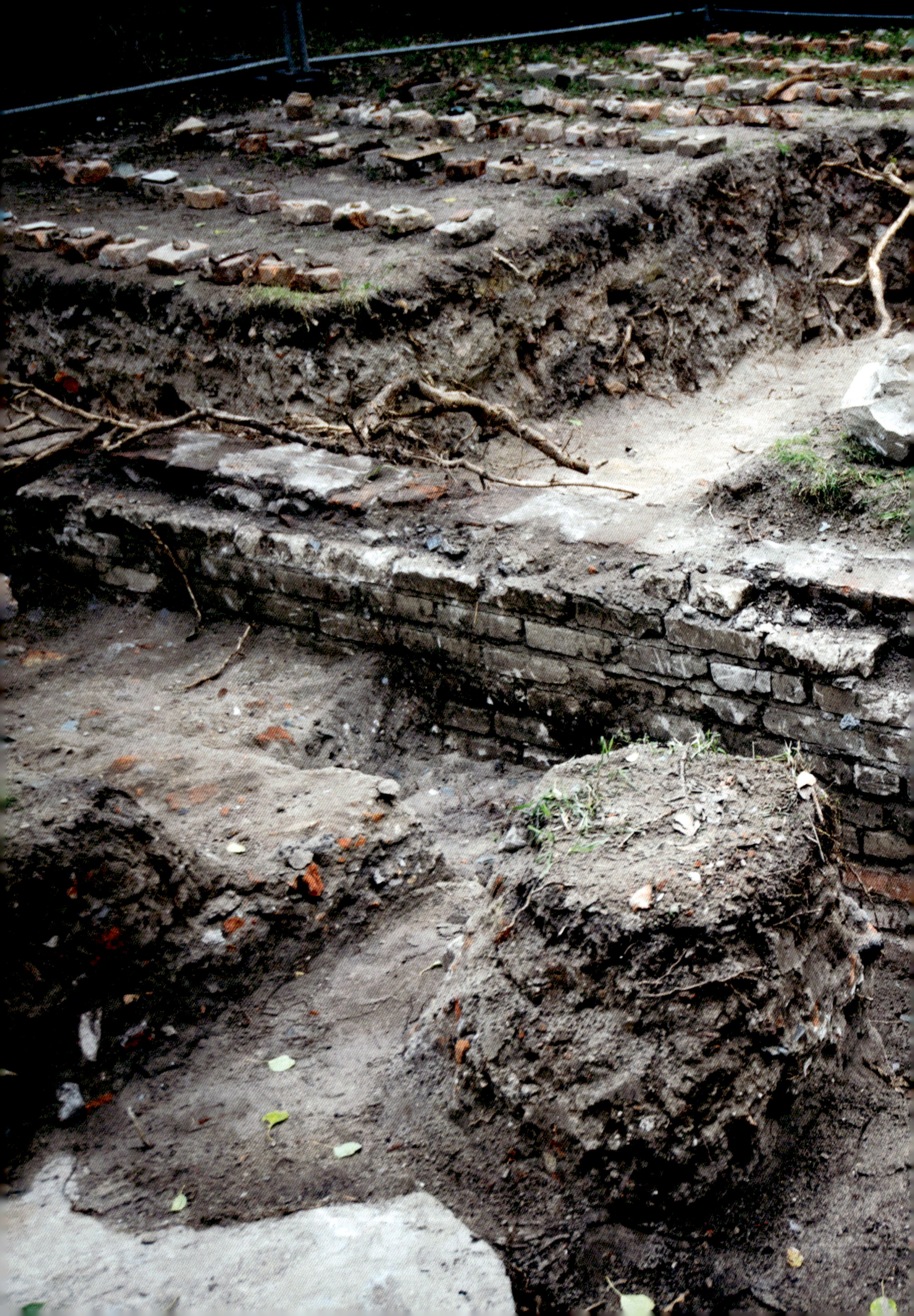